LIBERATION
and
RECONCILIATION

LIBERATION and RECONCILIATION

A Black Theology

Revised Edition

J. DEOTIS ROBERTS

ORBIS BOOKS

Maryknoll, New York 10545

The Catholic Foreign Mission Society of America (Maryknoll) recruits and trains people for overseas missionary service. Through Orbis Books, Maryknoll aims to foster the international dialogue that is essential to mission. The books published, however, reflect the opinions of their authors and are not meant to represent the official position of the society.

Library of Congress Cataloging-in-Publication Data

Roberts, J. Deotis (James Deotis), 1927-
    Liberation and reconciliation : a Black theology / J. Deotis
Roberts. — Rev. ed.
        p.   cm.
    Includes bibliographical references and index.
    ISBN 0-88344-951-X (pbk.)
    1. Black theology.   2. Race — Religious aspects — Christianity.
I. Title.
BT82.7.R59   1994
230'.08996 — dc20
                                                    93-38133
                                                      CIP

For
The late Principal Charles S. Duthie
New College, University of London
and Professor William L. Bradley
Rockefeller Foundation
friends and mentors

and for
The late Dean Emeritus Daniel G. Hill
Howard University School of Religion
who called me to the theological task.

These by their thought and life
introduced me to the liberating and
reconciling dimensions of Christian theology.

Contents

Preface to the First Edition

The present volume is an introduction to soul theology. Soul sums up the black experience, whether religious or secular, better than any other term. Here I have attempted a Christian theological interpretation of the soul religious experience as we understand it, as a Christian and as a theologian whose face is black. Soul theology is Black Theology.

Afro-American is my version of blackness. It includes a positive appreciation for the Euro-American contribution to black culture in this country. Afro-American does not, however, preclude the possibility that we will seek a deeper knowledge and understanding of Africanisms upon our experience. Thus while seeking to apply whatever insights I have gained from a comprehensive exposure to general theological knowledge, I am likewise attempting to correct the omissions regarding the uniqueness of black religious experience in most existent theological programs. In a word, theological knowledge is combined with black religious experience in Christian theological perspective.

In the following pages much will be said about black liberation. We are aware of the gospel of freedom to which Christ as Liberator has called us. But as Christians, black and white, we surely know that separation, however rewarding to set the record straight, cannot be an ultimate Christian goal. Separation must give way to reconciliation. The gospel is a reconciling as well as a liberating gospel, and Christ is at once Liberator and Reconciler. At the same time that black Christians are set free, they are called together with all other Christians to a ministry of reconciliation.

Reconciliation, between blacks and whites, is a two-way street. It depends as much upon what whites will do to make conditions in race relations better as it does upon what blacks will not do. Black-white reconciliation, in Christian terms, cannot be based upon the superordination-subordination pattern of whites over blacks. Whites must now be ready to work with blacks for better racial understanding. Reconciliation must be based upon a oneness in nature and grace between all people upon the principle of equity. Equality belongs to the time of integration.

Reconciliation assumes that blacks must earn the right to be equal—to be accepted into the American mainstream. Equity, on the other hand, belongs to the time of Black Power—black pride, awareness, and self-determination. Equity assumes that all human beings are naturally equal. Human dignity is a birthright. Black Theology affirms this and goes on to root equity, as the only principle of black-white reconciliation, in the Christian understanding of creation and redemption.

I am grateful to my colleagues in the Department of Religion at Swarthmore College for their assistance and encouragement. Professors Linwood Urban, Patrick Henry, and George Thomas (professor emeritus of Princeton University) were all helpful in their several ways. Mention must also be made of students at Swarthmore who provided a trial run for much of the material written here. Lectures at Swarthmore and Princeton, together with dialogues in the workshop on black religious experience at the 1969 annual session of the Religious Education Association, greatly accelerated progress on the manuscript. Frequent discussion with black colleagues on the theological commission of the National Committee of Black Churchmen has been enlightening. Lecture and dialogue at the first annual session of the Black Ecumenical Commission of Massachusetts contributed much to whatever clarity there may be in these pages.

The staff and consultants of the Westminster Press have been extremely helpful in the development and editing of the text. Mrs. Sylvia Hecht labored long and hard as typist to put the manuscript into acceptable form. I owe to my wife and children a debt that cannot be put into words. While I am grateful to all who assisted me, I hereby assume full responsibility for all the mistakes and shortcomings in the following pages. I will be pleased if the reader will consider the "end" of this book as a "beginning" toward liberation and reconciliation.

Preface to the 1994 Edition

Liberation and Reconciliation was first released in 1971. This was after a considerable period of gestation. Many thoughtful exchanges took place during 1968 and the following years. I will not repeat these influences here. There were many aspects to this development that were personal as well as societal. Happenings in both the church and the academy explain many ideas expressed as well as the passionate manner in which the material was presented. The years between 1968 and 1971 were filled with crises and rapid social change. Much that occurred at that time will not likely be repeated. And yet the impact of events of that period in U.S. race relations remains with us today.

Some Reasons for This Second Edition

In this new release of my foundational work in Black Theology, I attempt to preserve as much as possible the essential message of the original text. I also attempt to preserve the basic outlook of this work. In some cases it may be necessary to briefly indicate the historic context in order to make more explicit the significance of a particular observation and its meaning. But one of the compelling reasons for releasing this text at this time is the continuance and even the resurgence of white racism. The astute observer will conclude that the more things have changed in U.S. black-white relations the more they have remained the same.

Multicultural developments have emerged to such an extent that matters of human relations are more complicated than ever. Racial tensions have been intensified by a large influence of other nonwhite ethnics from the Southern hemisphere. It is unfortunate that more progress was not made in black-white relations before this more complicated situation developed. The tension is now at an epidemic stage between blacks and Hispanics, blacks and Asians, as well as others. Other nonwhite ethnic peoples are competing with blacks in urban America for limited resources.

Between 1971 and the present, the larger society has placed a moratorium on affirmative action initiatives. Law, custom, and executive actions have slowed the forward movement of progressive blacks. The black underclass has grown and has been overwhelmed by subtle forms of oppression.

Thus circumstances at present are ripe for a repeat of the message of this work, which has gone unheeded and unheard.

The message of Black Theology has not been properly considered on a large scale by black church leadership in the past. Fortunately, several seminary-educated men and women incorporate insights from this program in their ministries. Some scholarly pastors are beginning to interpret its benefits for those without formal theological education. A "second generation" of black as well as womanist theologians are insisting upon the merits of Black Theology in the church and the academy. The demand for available original workers on this subject is greater than ever before. Some pastors, upon reading works in Black Theology, indicate that what they are reading in new works depends largely upon foundational books written during the heyday of Black Theology. For these as well as other reasons, *Liberation and Reconciliation* is being reissued.

How and Why My Mind Has Changed or Remained the Same

First, there is no reason for a strong reaction to the theological position of Professor James H. Cone. Some critics in the past saw my views as mainly a personal response to the more radical views of Cone.

This criticism of my first systematic statement of Black Theology is not totally accurate. This appears to be so due to some very strong observations made concerning several important points in Cone's earlier books. There were basic disagreements between us and these were stated. In a review of the text, I am somewhat surprised by the extent to which these critical observations were lifted up.

However, the reader would miss the point dwelling upon these differences between Cone and myself. For example, there were forces at work that drove each black theologian forward. We were often in conversation and we often shared in the drafting of common statements. We shared much in the passion for racial justice.

At the outset, it was obvious that my role as a theologian antedated Cone's emergence at the peak of the Black Power movement. As a member of an earlier generation of theologians, I was influenced by the period of race relations impacted by the 1954 school decision, the Civil Rights Movement, and the nonviolent program of Dr. M. L. King, Jr. This long period of hindsight in the racial struggle for justice informed my message.

One has always to consider the autobiography of a theologian. We have different spiritual journeys, and intellectual and personal temperaments. Our experiences are very personal and racism has impacted us differently. Each theologian has a "life-story" that explains very much the direction of his or her theological reflection.

Not only my personal history, but my intellectual pilgrimage has been epistemological—a quest for a reasonable place for a stand. This had taken me into the history of ideas in the West. But it had also sent me on a global religious quest prior to my encounter with the issues presented by the black religious experience. My encounter with Euro-American religious thought had been deep on both sides of the Atlantic as well as in principal universities and divinity schools across this nation. It would not have been possible, therefore, to be in concert with Cone or merely react to what he had to say.

The text I produced was both a response to key issues raised by Cone and an alternative constructive statement of Black Theology. It is only if the latter purpose of *Liberation and Reconciliation* is taken seriously that one can fully appreciate its complete message.

I will now suggest how experience and reflection since 1971 would be present in a similar project today.

First, there is a greater sensitivity to the need to address a larger audience – the masses of poor-oppressed people. The underclass has increased and homelessness has multiplied. The scourge of drugs and wanton violence, so destructive to the young, has escalated out of control. The need to develop an even greater solidarity with the oppressed has become clear.

Black Theology must be a theology "from below." Black Theology must be addressed to all in a language they can understand. I see the need to simplify the message to reach a wider audience. However, it was necessary to work through the material much as it was first done. Without grappling with issues at the depth level, one is not able to tone it down and make it palatable for those with less formal education. Thus what needs to be done now is a second-order process. The message needs to reach more people.

In a similar vein, it is clear that Black Theology must be closely related to the black church. Its message needs to challenge all Christians, whether in pulpit or pew. Its goal is praxeological. Its purpose is social transformation for making life more human. Black Theology must become a theology of mission and ministry. The future and effectiveness of Black Theology is bound up with the witness of the black church. This fact becomes more and more apparent as we move forward in our history. The healing and protest aspects of the black church's mission are more and more evident.

Second, the balance between *liberation* and *reconciliation* remains essential in our pluralistic society. The multicultural emphasis now in vogue makes the urgency for genuine reconciliation more significant than before. The message of the Kerner report, which spoke of "two societies," black and white, has now been expanded to include other nonwhite ethnic groups. The so-called ethnic cleansing in Bosnia and the resurgence of antiforeign sentiments in a united Germany remind us of a tragic path we dare not take. Dr. King's warning, that we either learn to live together as friends or die as fools, is obvious for all thoughtful people.

When reconciliation is elevated to its proper ethical level and Christian understanding, it requires serious attention to liberation from social injustices. It cannot be conceived as mere sentimentality or "cheap grace." Reconciliation requires repentance, forgiveness, and cross-bearing. Thus I would opt for maintaining the balance between liberation and reconciliation. At the same time, I would invite others to seriously rethink the meaning of both terms in light of the new challenges in human relations associated with racial and ethnic tensions in this last decade of the twentieth century.

Third, there is the message of Black Theology for the entire human family. As theologies become more contextualized, Black Theology stands out as a powerful message for oppressed people. The location of Black Theology in the heart of the First World, on behalf of a group who experience much of the deprivation of persons in the Third World, makes its impact the more meaningful. Blacks have significant contact with Euro-American culture. But their ancestry is African. Black Theology, as much as Latin American Liberation Theology, has a vital message for the oppressed everywhere. The relation to the South African racial situation is obvious. Through personal encounter and dialogue, I can affirm the impact of Black Theology upon Dalit Theology in India and Minjung Theology in South Korea, to name only two instances. Thus since 1971 I have become more and more aware of the global influence of Black Theology. However, the influence of other theologies among oppressed people enriches and empowers Black Theology as well.

Fourth, the use of inclusive language is an obvious change in this text. The sexism in the first edition is offensive to the present writer. Thus this is perhaps the most radical change that has occurred since the earlier attempt to state my position as a theology of the black experience. The language used earlier was presented without the benefit of conversation and writings by feminist and womanist theologians.

While the language is important it does not equal the importance of a new sense of relationship. That is to say, there needs to be a conviction that women are equal partners with men through nature and grace.

As I have worked through the text to clean up the language, I have attempted to rethink the proper manner to assert the equality, partnership, and mutuality between the sexes. Without this latter effort, the use of inclusive language can be useless and meaningless. Without an equal partnership, change of language is useless.

As a black male theologian, perhaps the most significant development has been the emergence of Womanist Theology. Black women, in relation to men and children, share a common context, in which they have been able to share their pain. They have shown much understanding and compassion for black men, who assumed that they had spoken about liberation for all black people a few decades ago. In the meantime, I have sensed a significant growth in the comprehension of the issues raised by these theological reflections of men and women together.

The time has come for criticism to move in two directions and not just from women to men, but from men to women as well. Thus I am concerned that womanist theologians have not, to my knowledge, devoted as much time to the black family as black male theologians have. This is rather odd in view of the crucial role that black women play in the nurture of all children, male and female. Strong families are so important to our health and survival as a people that Womanist Theologians need to make their important contribution on this front. Most black women I know care a lot about family; it is therefore important that their sisters who are theologians should give some guidance on this subject. It is obvious that a lot of the poverty of black women is due to their assuming responsibilities related to the rearing of children. How then is it possible to deal with "class" oppression of black women without serious attention to family?

This is a large and vital subject, now before us. Unfortunately, many black male pastors have not moved forward against the oppression of women, especially in the church and in ministry. It is the more tragic that their status quo position is sanctioned by a wrongful interpretation of scripture. Male black theologians, however, appear to be very supportive of all women in their bid for equal status with men in church and society. Black male theologians have often taken a lot of heat for their convictions from male ministerial colleagues. In spite of this, we must use whatever influence we have to support the equality and partnership of women. This must be done at the same time that we champion the cause of the young black male, black families, and especially all black youth.

Fifth, there is a need for a definitive theology of ministry out of the black church tradition. I believe this can be more effectively done by those who have chosen full-time ministry, even though they have contributed to theological reflection. Persons like Delores Carpenter and James H. Harris are applying the insights of black and womanist theologies for their work as effective pastors. I see their work as the most effective way of validating the message of black men and women theologians. The witness of Ben Chavis, new executive director of the NAACP, demonstrates the significance of black theology in the area of public policy. Delores and Ben are former students of mine. Thus I have grounds for assessing the extent to which Black Theology informs their life and work. The future use of the insights of Black Theology in ministry and the quest for social justice appear promising.

Contextualizing the Message of Black Theology

It is not necessary to do all the updating of my original text here, since I have done much of this in books, essays, and articles since this book was first released.

In 1974 I published *A Black Political Theology*. The purpose of that work was to make clearer my focus on liberation as a goal. That work also was more "ethical" in perspective. *Liberation and Reconciliation* was more in the nature of constructive theology.

Roots of a Black Future was released in 1980. This was a treatise on the black church and family. This study was on the extended family tradition from Africa to the New World. This interdisciplinary study included much history and social science. But it was grounded in scripture and theology. Its ultimate purpose was to provide a theology for ministry to black families.

Black Theology Today saw the light of day in 1983. This was a collection of essays on the development of black theology in my own awareness. But even more so it was a critical evaluation of the works of several colleagues in the field.

In 1987 *Black Theology in Dialogue* appeared as a more global presentation. It argued for the maturity and status of Black Theology worldwide. It consisted of essays and lectures presented in conversations in several parts of the world.

At the present time, I await the release of a new volume that relates Black Theology to the practice of ministry. This anticipated volume focuses upon the "prophetic" message for black churches in their social justice ministries. I am aware of a need for Black Theology to address the healing aspect of the gospel in the witness of the churches as well. It is my conviction that the *holistic* perspective of the gospel of Jesus Christ is native to the black church tradition. Thus a black church theology needs to explicate a holistic message.

This brief summary is limited to books; it does not include articles and essays. The reader is to be reminded that much of my reflection is much broader than the black experience.

This summary of major works that I have produced since releasing *Liberation and Reconciliation* should provide the reader with guidelines for judging the direction the germinal insights of the earlier work have developed in my life and thought.

How Events Have Created New Perspectives

Here I attempted to look at each chapter and lift up certain matters that might now be viewed differently.

Chapter 1 treats of "theological discourse." The mood is very passionate in keeping with the challenge before the black community. "Black consciousness" and "black power" dominated the mode of expression. "Black" had a special meaning, which had developed in the late 1960s, during the long hot summer of racial strife.

While the same problems of racism confront us today, the mood is more subdued and the language is less passionate. Many people who never grasped the meaning of "blackness" now see themselves as African-American. Some of us can accept the new title, but it has greater meaning if one has first understood the significance of the "blackness" content of the earlier period. It had to do with self-esteem and empowerment, without which there can be no real freedom for black people.

Chapter 2 opens up the meaning of the title *Liberation and Reconciliation*. In this chapter an attempt was made to treat the options before the black community and the nation. On the one hand, there were the black nationalists. Some were religious and sought liberation through a separation of the races. Liberation was to be by "whatever means necessary." This included violence as a means to liberation. On the other hand, there were persons among us who were willing to be "reconciled" with whites based upon their understanding of the gospel as a gospel of "love" only. They were willing to allow whites to teach them what to believe. The often Bible-based gospel knew nothing of justice in the here and now. It was often an individualistic and otherworldly gospel.

The attempt was made to present both liberation and reconciliation as a balance within the gospel message. It seemed to me that both were part of the black church tradition and that the gospel required both outlooks as well. It is likely that a part of my insight harked back to the Civil Rights and nonviolent movements. But I was also very much a part of the new more militant stance of black power. Thus there was an attempt to delve deep in both outlooks and pull them together. I reserved the right to seek my own definitions of both terms. While rejecting integration based upon the inferior-superior formula, I was open to reconciliation between equals. I was open to goodwill, but insisted on structural changes in the social arrangements between blacks and whites. Thus I saw the relation between liberation and reconciliation as dialectical, but not oppositional. The struggle to bring these two poles together has been a challenge ever since. Sincerely raising this issue provided significant options and challenges for the whole black theology/church movement. For the devout believer there is no easy answer.

Chapter 3 delved deeply into our African heritage as well as the African-American past in this country. Observing the manner in which individualism had dealt a divisive wedge between black persons, I lifted up "peoplehood" as an essential outlook for blacks in quest of freedom and justice.

Much of this chapter deals with the "chosen people" paradigm as applied to the destiny of blacks. At that time it was possible to focus on the tension between the races in the U.S.A. Today the issue is not as clear. With the breakup of the U.S.S.R. and the trend toward "ethnic cleansing" in Bosnia, not to mention the rise of multiculturalism in our country, there is a need to give serious attention to what humans have in common to live fulfilled lives in the same country, in the same world. Some similar insights are valuable, but the historical and sociological contexts have changed since the book was first released.

Chapter 4 treats the doctrine of God. My view on God remains the same. It has not been easy to use inclusive language. Some statements may appear awkward in view of my own struggle with new words and concepts. I do see some enrichment in overcoming the male-only designation of the divine nature. It is here that the reflections of womanist theologians will be most helpful. We black male theologians will need to continue vigorous conversation with womanist theologians and feminist theologians as well.

Chapter 5 is an important statement on human dignity out of the human experience. This emphasis is still needed. However, there seems to be great need for stress on "self-esteem" for the black youth of this present period. We are faced with an epidemic of drugs and violence, and a growing underclass. The recovery of the drive for self-fulfillment of earlier black generations needs to be a priority. The general message of chapter 5 regarding sin and forgiveness stands. However, the presence of the religious right indicates a need to give careful attention to the meaning of liberation in the overcoming of sin and the experience of salvation. We need to be precise in indicating what concerns and actions contribute to social justice. Are the issues of the majority our issues? Roman Catholics and conservative Evangelicals are united against abortion, for example. While seeing the serious nature of the outlook of "abortion on demand," this does not tackle the serious problems caused by systematic racism. More than ever, Black Theology must lead black Christians in their own thinking and living out of the faith.

The issues raised in chapter 6 regarding the black messiah remain crucial. This discussion is related to the discussions going on in third-world theologies on "the images of Jesus." In a way, Black Theology anticipated this development. The subject is still alive among black religious thinkers. For example, Father James Stallings, who founded his own African-American Catholic communion, continues this vital discussion. The discussion has been enriched by the research and reflection of black biblical scholars, women as well as men. The earlier discussion is greatly illuminated by recent reflections and writings. The christological reflections of Professor Jacquelyn Grant are to be noted.

The chapter on hope (chap. 7) is always important to theology. It becomes even more important as the black underclass grows. The balance between the concern for the "here" and "hereafter" presented in the earlier essay should stand. I would still insist that the Christian faith's belief in the resurrection-event empowers our moral endeavors in this life—both personal and social. Many things have happened during the intervening years, which would be used to place this message in context. The moratorium on active programs for the upligft of the poor as well as blacks has made more emphatic the need to relate eschatology to ethics. We know the awful negative effects of the Reagan-Bush years. The promises of President Clinton remain to be kept. The words of Jesus, "thy kingdom come, on earth as it is in heaven," are an appropriate challenge for black Christians—and for all Christians.

Chapter 8 reveals more than any other chapter the historical context of this book. It was born of the attempt to address the challenge presented by the "by-any-means-necessary" ethic so often advocated at the time. As the recent explosions in Los Angeles and Miami indicate, this outlook is not fully overcome. Racism is not dead; it reappears again and again in various times and places. It presents new challenges each day. How we deal with the consequences of racism remains central to black faith. With this comes the challenge presented by the title of this volume — *Liberation and Reconciliation*.

In this new Introduction I have attempted to update a new generation of readers regarding the message of this early volume in Black Theology. Without opening up the text in a way that would destroy its "classic" flavor, I have made these additional remarks. A select bibliography is being presented to aid those who desire a fuller update. Many of these sources have informed me in the series of volumes I have produced since this book was first released.

It has been by the request of several younger black theologians that this volume has been reissued. I wish to acknowledge the warm reception of this proposal by Robert Ellsberg, Editor-in-Chief of Orbis Books. Without his encouragement and skillful editing, this volume might have remained in oblivion, as far as younger readers are concerned.

I would also like to thank Mirta I. Angleró, faculty secretary at Eastern Baptist Theological Seminary, for her tireless and efficient preparation of this text. It is my fondest desire to make this work available to laity and clergy alike. The message of this book remains alive whenever Christians seek to live by the gospel, which both liberates and reconciles us to God and each other.

LIBERATION
and
RECONCILIATION

1

Theological Discourse in Black

The current concern for writing down a Black Theology provides an opportunity for black theologians to do their own thing. I now have the opportunity to say some things I would have said several years ago. The course of events in race relations, however, has led me to change my mind so suddenly and so radically most recently that it would not have been possible for me to have anticipated the new direction my thought is now taking. I must say, nevertheless, that apart from the development, the hindsight, and common sense of past years of maturation as a general practitioner in the field of theology, the present and future direction of my thought would be different.

Every theologian arrives at his or her stance through years of reflection. There is an autobiography of thought that emerges, however objective and critical one attempts to be. I stand somewhere between the generations — that is, on the boundary between the black militants and the old-fashioned civil rights integrationist — and also between the "by-whatever-means-necessary" ethicists and the view that ends and means are organically one. It is my view that liberation and reconciliation must be considered at the same time and in relation to each other. The all-or-nothing, victory-or-death, approach to race relations appears to be more rhetoric than reality, even to those who hold it. The same may be said concerning the black or white conception of ethics. In the long run, gray is more honest and realistic.

How Black Is Black Theology?

There is one thing that black theologians do not need to decide; it has been already decided for them. Their face is black in a white racist society. This racism is institutionalized not only in the general society but in the church as well. Black consciousness or awareness is a realistic foundation for our theological task. When blacks move from color blindness to color consciousness, it becomes difficult to avoid the implications of Black Power.

Black Power has psychological, sociological, economic, political, and religious implications. The black theologian needs to take into account all these factors that shape human life.

The black theologian is free, however, to decide how he or she will interpret black experience. He or she is obligated to provide an understanding of black consciousness, black pride, black self-determination—in a word, Black Power. He or she must seek to be faithful to the believing community, as a theologian. But he or she is required, at the same time, to give a helpful interpretation of the Christian faith to those who honestly seek to be their true black selves and Christian at the same time.

The black theologian has an ethical question to treat. Christianity, like all the great religions, has a built-in ethic. No theologian of this believing community can escape the ethical questions raised by racism, whether white oppression or black response. A theologian of an ethical religion must consider the ethical concerns of religion as being within the scope of reflection. A God of love, justice, and mercy, and a humble walk with Godself, can be understood only in the light of theological ethics. The Christian God as Creator, Redeemer, and Judge can be fully understood through a careful reflection upon God's moral attributes.

Black theologians cannot excuse themselves from the task of doing theological ethics by pointing out the moral hypocrisy of white Christians. Their neglect of the ethical requirements of the Christian faith has gotten us in the impasse we now face in race relations. If, as Christians, we are to overcome the present tragic situation in race relations, some group needs to point to the true ethical demands of the Christian faith. Unfaithfulness, hypocrisy, and irresponsibility are obviously not the answer—white Christians have made this unmistakably clear. The National Committee of Black Christians is correct in speaking of "conscience." But is "revenge" our only proper response to the evil done us? If love is blind, hate can see no better. Dr. Martin Luther King, Jr.'s, question haunts us still. It must be dealt with by black theologians in a serious manner. "Where do we go from here—chaos or community?"

A persistent question is: What is a Black Theology? Sometimes the question is raised as if it were a *bête noire.* Most often the question is asked with the assumption that a Black Theology is juxtaposed to a "white" theology, and is, therefore, racist in outlook. Naturally the question is usually posed by whites who think in racist terms and who surmise that blacks are about to turn the tables. On the other hand, blacks, for the most part, have no racist intention—they assume that there is latent, unwritten Black Theology, which now needs to be recorded. Therefore, the black Christian is greatly concerned and deeply anxious that those who are trained in theology assume this task. We are urged on in this matter—the mandate is from the people. In this work, I am assuming a personal measure of this responsibility.

I am assuming from the outset that there is a Black Theology and that it provides its own context and language. We have before us an eternal gospel, communicated through scripture, tradition, and the witness of the Spirit in Christian life through the ages. This is the "givenness" of revelation that most critics fear black Christians are now prepared to surrender. But we have, at the same time, a context of thought: life and belief in which the Christian faith must be "appropriated," adapted, or understood — this is our black religious experience.

Here Tillich's "boundary" concept is helpful. But where he was greatly concerned about the dialogue between philosophy and theology, the black theologian may find the dialogue between the humanities, behavioral sciences, and the "live" black religious tradition more helpful. Black Christians are caught up in a "dialect of survival" in a racist society. The black Christian is concerned about the relation between faith and life. His or her "ultimate concern" has to do with life-and-death decisions. His or her "situation" is the racism that affects the total life and the experiences of his or her loved ones.

Is it possible to project a meaningful theological, ethical, and pragmatic stance where one has been neither tested nor tried? Can one who is committed to one set of values sincerely follow any change without raising serious questions? What is the role and place of experience? Is it not to be expected that persons taught by life itself will be more cautious and critical of novelty? Can one who has been convinced by the Christian faith as a way of life suddenly abandon this lifestyle and embrace, without question, a "revenge and revolt" approach to race relations? Can an apostle of love turn, all of a sudden, to being an apostle of hate and sprinkle "holy water" upon the most unauthentic, racist, pathological, irresponsible, and violent approaches to racial change? Can there be a constructive interpretation of this new militancy, which can be reinterpreted and even sponsored by the Christian faith with its revolutionary message? It is the opinion of this author that the latter is possible and that this is the proper mission of a Black Theology.

Black/Black and Black/White Communication

Interpretation, *hermeneutike*, has to do with the use of language in the understanding of truth. Hermeneutics is now being used in theology to indicate more than is implied by interpretation — as speech, translation, and commentary. It also has to do with communication that is possible when normal communication breaks down due to some serious impediment to understanding. Hermeneutics, therefore, refers to an attempt on the part of people to understand one another and make themselves understood.[1] Charles Long is correct, I believe, when he refers to the race problem as a "hermeneutical" task.[2] It is one that deserves interpretation. The interpretation of the black religious experience in terms of the Christian creed is the mission of Black Theology.

Theology is God-talk. The word "theology" is derived from two Greek words: *theos*, which means "God," and *logos*, which means "reasoning" or "thinking." Thus theology is "reasoning about God." In the study of theology, we have two key words: "God" and "thinking." If there are no atheists in foxholes, it may likewise be said that few blacks have been afforded the luxury of disbelieving in the divine existence. The existence of God does not, therefore, need to be established through the several "proofs," and a Black Theology may begin with a primary faith that God is. The problem of God, for blacks, has more to do with the divine character.

Much of the raw material of Black Theology will be intuitive. We have to do to a great extent with an "unwritten" body of doctrine. For much of its history, the black church was "an invisible institution." Even "the black presence" has yet to be fully treated in theological terms. But this does not mean that the theological task for the black theologian is futile or that there is no body of material for examination.

Black religion is an integral part of the black experience. Most black historians, not being inclined toward theology, have not done justice to the black religious experience. Without a real appreciation for religious phenomena, black historians, sociologists, and anthropologists have not done justice to the religious heritage of blacks. The abundance of raw materials for Black Theology is overwhelming. Among the sources that may be freighted with religious insights we may list literature, history, sermons, spirituals, folklore, art, and the testimony of some saints and sages of the black community. All these feed into a Black Theology that is a process of reasoning about God in the context of the black experience.

It is Richard N. Soulen's opinion that hermeneutical theology supplies the categories for the illumination of all Christian worship and not merely the black church. The history of the black church and of black worship is largely an oral tradition. He, therefore, points to the need to gather data and reflect theologically on forms and modes of worship in the black church to discover which aspects of black worship speak most meaningfully the language of the Christian faith. In sum, Soulen says:

> This is not for the sake of the black church alone; it is for the sake of the whole church. For not until white middle class Christians come to understand the language and modes of black worship are they likely to understand either the black church or its people. And perhaps not until then will they truly understand themselves.[3]

In my judgment Soulen has provided some helpful guidelines for inter-communication between blacks and whites as blacks reflect theologically upon the Afro-American Christian tradition. However, it is my belief that he has taken the delimitations of James Cone too seriously.[4] As a white scholar, he may not desire to take exception to Cone's position, but the narrowness that Cone has sought to impose upon Black Theology must be rejected. This must be done for the sake of Black Theology itself. If we unwisely mark off a little space for our operation as black scholars, most white scholars will gladly let us operate only within these bounds. There will be no need to admit the black theologian to the comprehensive field of theology. Some of us have fought too long and hard to give up this territory now.

There is also the need for intercommunication if there is to be reconciliation between blacks and whites. While Cone confesses an indifference toward whites, I care. It is my concern that a language event and a language gain occur as I reflect as a theologian upon the black religious experience. It is my desire to speak to blacks and whites separately, but in the long run it is hoped that real intercommunication between blacks and whites may result from this hermeneutical program.

Communication between blacks and whites is hampered by lack of sensitivity and urgency, by procrastination and playing games on the part of many whites. Blacks, on the other hand, if they really understand their plight, are deadly serious. They have life-and-death decisions to make. They are caught up in the "dialectic of survival." Race relations are characterized by paralysis of will. There is a need for "obedient love." Compassion, empathy — love in action — is needed. Sympathy, pity, or passive concern are inadequate. The gospel demands radical obedience. Salvation means decision, committing the whole self to God in the concrete situation. The kingdom claims us now in obedience. In radical obedience, love of God is entwined with love of neighbor. Such "radical obedience" is needed in the field of race.

Those of us who have black skin and who are conscious of our blackness, but who have passed through various stages of racial protest, face a problem of "internal communication" with young, angry, militant black youth who have just discovered what it means to be black in a white racist society. There is a great deal of religious motivation behind black militancy and black nationalism. Many blacks who are not Christians are associated with "the religion of Black Power." A black theologian who operates from the Christian faith has difficulty being heard in this company, however angry he may be. Vincent Harding is the brain trust of this Black Power religion. James Cone is on the fence between the Christian faith and the religion of Black Power. It will be necessary for Cone to decide presently where he will take his firm stand. The present writer takes his stand within the Christian theological circle.

A Christian theologian is not an interpreter of the religion of Black Power. He or she, as black theologian, may be the interpreter of Afro-American Christianity. He or she may be in tune with the meaning of Black Power. But he or she is attempting to understand the Christian faith in the light of his or her people's experience. This task is not popular. One runs the risk of being misunderstood by black militants and moderates as well as by white radicals and liberals. The only encouragement is the urgency and need arising from the new situation. The religious need is latent and even unconscious for many blacks, but the black theologian senses a clear mandate to engage in the challenge ahead.

This theological task is a type of ministry to blacks and whites. It is a priestly ministry of blacks. As one speaks of deliverance, one can bring comfort and assurance to those who have been victimized by inhuman treatment much too long. But to many blacks, reconciliation will come as harsh judgment. The black theologian's role is that of a prophet as well. His or her message will often be unwelcomed by blacks as well as by whites. But insofar as one speaks the Christian message in the area of race, one will need to speak of reconciliation beyond confrontation and liberation, whatever the risk and whatever the personal cost.

The worldview of native Africans and black Americans is not the same. This is true even if both are Christians. My understanding of the Christian faith, after taking under careful consideration the African heritage, is clearly Afro-American. There are similarities, but there are fundamental differences as well. Africans and American blacks often find themselves on the same wavelength. There seems to be real communication between blacks and Africans beyond any understanding that whites may have of either blacks or Africans. But three hundred fifty years is a long time to be exiled in a "strange land." Between blacks and Mother Africa there is considerable temporal and spatial distance. This distance is social, cultural, and historical to the extent that there is a fundamental difference between the African and the Afro-American.

We must consider what America has done *to* the blacks in this country as well as what America has done *for* blacks. Consider the repression and destruction of the African heritage and institutions, especially family life and religion. This is a hint at what America has done to black people.

We may still have the African temperament or an Oriental mind. We have retained many Africanisms, but the cultural context in which we have developed is Euro-American. The Judeo-Christian, Greco-Roman milieu has colored our entire outlook and shaped our worldview. Our history in this country has a hold upon us—we cannot leap over the centuries. Our past and our present are Afro-American. In spite of all the difficulties involved in this affirmation, we will need to deal with this reality. In a real sense we are dealing with a Christian theological and ethical understanding of Afro-American thought and tradition.

It is true that primary experience is a prerequisite to in-depth under-standing of any faith claim. This leads Cone to say that only the oppressed may write or understand a theology of oppression. But my study of world religions as well as ecumenical theology lead me to hold a broader view. It is possible to study a faith-claim from the inside, but it is also possible to understand a faith-claim from the "outside." The inside study is necessary, but it is often too subjective to be sufficiently critical and evaluative. The outside study may be supplementary by being more objective and by bringing careful analysis and critical judgment to bear upon an affirmation of faith. An anthropologist or philosopher with a positivistic or humanistic understanding of all phenomena may sit loose to religious affirmations. A theologian, however, studying the faith of other believers can somehow appreciate the inside of another faith-claim because of what one's own means. A real fellow feeling, empathy, or rapport emerges as a truly interreligious encounter takes place among theologians who are devotees of several religions.

A Black Theology that takes reconciliation seriously must work at the task of intercommunication between blacks and whites under the assumption that for those who are open to truth, there may be communication from the inside out, but at the same time there may be communication from the outside in. In the latter sense, white Christians may be led to understand and work with blacks for liberation and reconciliation on an interracial basis.

Black and white Christians have been living an unauthentic life in this country in the area of race. Whites have ignored the requirements of "love, justice, and mercy." They are guilty of malpractice as Christians; they have been hypocritical and involved in double-dealing in the area of race. Words and deeds have been antithetical. Dishonesty and indifference have been common among whites even in integrated congregations and denominational bodies. White Christians have been living and behaving thus in an unauthentic manner. Black Christians who have passively accepted the blunt end of the misinterpretation and malpractice of white Christians have also lived an unauthentic existence. It is the goal of a worthy Black Theology to lead both blacks and whites to an authentic Christian existence.

The true life of faith should be for whites one that would enable them to accept all humans as equal to themselves. Black Christians are to be led to true self-understanding, self-respect, true personhood, and fulfillment as children of God. Because it is a liberating as well as a reconciliating theology, it combines meaning with protest. Confrontation, empowerment, and development programs may be the means whereby blacks will move to an authentic life. Therefore, not only the existential posture, but the ministry of Black Power may figure in a theological reflection upon the black experience. Authentic life for blacks is a movement through liberation to reconciliation. Authentic life for whites is a movement through humaneness to reconciliation. Reconciliation between blacks and whites must henceforth be in "deed and in truth"; it must be through humaneness and liberation, and it must be between equals.

These are prime objectives of a black theologian's reflections upon the Afro-American religious experience. Any black separatism, though arising directly from white resistance, must be understood as a "strategic withdrawal" for unity and empowerment, and not as permanent. Authentic existence for blacks and whites can only be realized finally in reconciliation between equals in the body of Christ.

2

Liberation and Reconciliation

Liberation and reconciliation are the two main poles of Black Theology. They are not antithetical—one moves naturally from one to the other in the light of the Christian understanding of God and humanity. The use of the words "liberation" and "reconciliation" is deliberate. It is obvious that I could speak of "freedom" instead of "liberation." Unfortunately, freedom has been so "white-washed," misapplied, delimited, and discriminating in usage in America that it has little meaning of importance for blacks. In a real sense, the words from the Declaration of Independence have different meanings for black and white Americans: "We hold these truths to be self-evident, that all men are created equal, that they are endowed by their Creator with certain unalienable Rights, that among these are Life, Liberty and the Pursuit of Happiness." Blacks might well raise a question—an existential question—at the conclusion of each affirmation. For example: "That all men created equal" (but me?).

Liberation is Marxist or socialist in ring. White Americans have a pathological fear of Marxism. White Americans say their fear of communism is the main reason why they are in Vietnam. The expansion of the war into other parts of Indochina is explained in like manner. Fascism is something else. This may be endorsed as a means of keeping blacks and radicals in tow. Freedom sums up what is. Liberation is revolutionary—for blacks it points to what ought to be. Black Christians desire radical and rapid social change in America as a matter of survival. Black Theology is a theology of liberation. We believe that the Christian faith is avowedly revolutionary and, therefore, it may speak to this need with great force.

Reconciliation is also crucial. Since "black nationalism" is a fantasy more akin to rhetoric than to reality, there is a common sense reason why reconciliation must be a postrevolutionary goal. But there is a theological basis for this reconciliation "between equals" as well, with which Black Theology should deal. Things being as they are in the racial crisis in America, there must be a "revolution." Black Theology is interested in what results from this radical and rapid change—whether chaos or community.

8

We have seen that many WASPs are good law-and-order-without-justice people. They prefer repression to any form of "black expression." They, we have observed, hate communism, but they are sure that fascism is in order if it maintains the status quo—"if it keeps the Niggers in their place." There may, then, be revolution without reconciliation. This may be true if a violent expression of Black Power is responded to by a white backlash in the form of massive police brutality. But there can be a revolution in race relations with reconciliation. This goal must be sought by black and white Christians together. What I am seeking is a Christian theological approach to race relations that will lead us beyond a hypocritical tokenism to liberation as a genuine reconciliation between equals.

Dr. Martin Luther King, Jr., could be pragmatic as well as moral as he spoke of nonviolence. He insisted that the choice in international relations, in an atomic age, is not between war and peace, but between nonviolence and nonexistence. He might have said almost the same thing about black-white relations in this country. What I have to say about reconciliation is to challenge men and women from apathy to action. But as far as blacks are concerned, whites may no longer be lieutenants but buck privates in the black community. They, however, may work at full potential in their own community to prepare their white neighbors for accepting blacks as people in a pluralistic or multiracial society.

The drifting apart of the races presents a difficult challenge to the black theologian interested in reconciliation, as it does to the entire Christian church in America. Polarization must be overcome, for it exists in the churches as it does in the total society. Among whites many "tired liberals" have joined the law-and-order-without-justice people. Many blacks have abandoned civil rights and joined the angry black separatists. Both need to consider the meaning of liberation in the context of reconciliation.

It is only through vigorous protest—a crisis—precipitating interpretation of theology that the Christian faith, speaking and acting in and through the black church and the black community, may spark the revolution that may yet liberate all black people in this crisis-response society. But beyond liberation we chart the guidelines for a true Christian reconciliation. If we are warned that reconciliation is too futuristic for consideration at this time, we reply to our critics that in the nature of our faith we must always seek reconciliation. Christianity is rooted in the belief that "God was in Christ reconciling the world to Godself" (2 Cor. 5:19), and that reconciliation between God and humans can be effected only through reconciliation between persons.

The exodus provides a central category for interpreting not only the Old Testament but the work of Jesus and the mission of the church as well. The exodus was an event in which a people experienced unexpected deliverance from bondage that came about through the breaking of the power of the oppressor. It meant the opening up of an until-then impossible future for those who had been oppressed.

In the history of Israel, the exodus became the paradigmatic event that provided the basic principle of interpretation of God's action in the life of the nation. It opened the way not only for the prophets but for a full development of eschatological and apocalyptic perspectives. It provided the resources for Jesus' understanding of life and mission, as well as for the interpretation of it that emerged in the apostolic church. Jesus' vision of the Kingdom of God is set in the context of imminent historical judgment; the resurrection is an act of creation *ex nihilo* and is thus a profound scandal for the world. In the words of Paul, it was the work of the God "who gives life to the dead and calls into existence the things that do not exist" (Rom. 4:17). This is essentially the view of the exodus presented by Einar Billing, Swedish theologian and bishop.[1] The exodus has been so meaningful to black Christians, perhaps it is a good starting point for a Black Theology.

According to von Rad, the central element in the judgments of the prophets upon the present order was that Yahweh would bring about a new era for his people.[2] They had freedom in dealing with the past. The new word often contradicted what had been proclaimed earlier, but Yahweh was seen as acting in the same way. Old religious institutions had become invalid. The prophets denounced and abandoned not only old social and political structures, but the fixed religious order as well. The break with the past is so great that there is discontinuity—the new state beyond cannot be seen as a continuation of what went before. God is "doing a new thing" (Isa. 43:19). Salvation is associated with a new action in history. Thus, the prophets seek meaning in contemporary events by looking forward to events planned in the sovereign freedom in God. The preaching of the apostles was characterized by an unrivaled ability to respond to new historical developments and to point toward the eventual appearance of the qualitatively new, a new entry into the land, the appearance of a new David, a new Zion, a new covenant.[3]

The question of "old wine and new wineskins" is at the heart of Black Theology. New wine must be produced in the area of race, but will the old wineskins contain it? Will the old white-controlled power structures contain new wine—Black Power, black self-determination, and human equality? Can the institutional church withstand such a radical change? If the old institutions (social, political, economic, religious, and cultural) cannot contain this "new wine," what must be the nature and structure of the "new wineskins"?

It is my view that the relation between the old order in race relations and the new is one of discontinuity. But I also see the need for continuity. The best of the past may be the matrix for launching the future. Jesus' assertion that his program was "fulfillment" rather than "destruction" of the old religious order is suggestive. Biblical faith is a movement from promise to fulfillment. But the church, as the new Israel, is related to the old Israel in terms of continuity-discontinuity. Christians in looking at Judaism often assume that "the child is father of the man." If they are honest, however, they must deal with the debt the Christian faith owes to Jewish history. Without a real appreciation of the old Israel, one cannot fully understand the new Israel. Continuity is a meaningful context for dealing with the discontinuity of the church vis-à-vis the Israel of the old covenant. This continuity-discontinuity paradigm is helpful in the treatment of the black religious experience, all racial questions, and the questions facing the larger society.

While creating an ideology for radical changes in race relations, I see the need for changes to be made within historical-institutional structures. But the changes are to be "root and branch" on the order of surgery rather than the application of salves to wounds with deep internal causes. For example, concerned white Christians engaged in charity work in black communities could render a more effective service through the humanizing and redirection of white power. One of the reasons why the District of Columbia finds home rule so difficult to obtain is that two-thirds of the population in the city are black. Often the chairman of the D.C. committee is a Southerner determined to promote white supremacy. The District of Columbia is a captive city of powerless blacks directly under the control of such individuals. While such congressmen are always pleased to point to the crime, illiteracy, illegitimacy, and other social ills common to all urban situations, they are not willing to pass and implement the kind of bills that will deal with the causes of these ills. White Christians and white voters in the several states can make home rule and such legislation possible.

The general biblical background of promise and fulfillment provides the context for the relationship between revelation and revolution. The categories of exodus, messianism, incarnation, and death/resurrection represent this relationship. To recognize revelation as decisively revolutionary in its character is to opt for the risk of commitment to radical change.[4] Bruce O. Boston reminds us that, in the exodus, revelation becomes revolution. He says:

> In the exodus the tyranny of the given was dethroned, for the children of Israel recognized that what can be is worth the risk of what is.[5]

The priority consideration at present is liberation for blacks. Whites and blacks who desire to aid in the liberation of blacks must understand the new agenda. The new agenda is written by blacks. Cone is correct—only the oppressed may write the agenda for their liberation. My concern is that the agenda be authentic according to a theological understanding of God and humanity.

Liberation is the theme of Black Theology. Christ is the liberator and the Christian faith promises "deliverance to the captives." It promises to let the oppressed go free. It follows, then, that any meaningful relationship between blacks and whites at this time will need to involve a give-and-take relationship of mutual cultural enrichment. Christians who have had so much to say about love and human understanding should lead in cross-cultural exchanges between blacks and whites. If this is to be done deeply and fully, there is required "desegregated hearts." Time has run out for game-playing, role-playing. "Judgment begins at the house of the Lord."

Often when the race question comes to the surface in a conversation with whites, it is made known that "I have a very dear friend who is black." The question is asked: "Do you know so and so?" Sometimes the person is virtually unknown. At other times the person is well known. In all cases the suggestion is made that if you know one black person, then all is well. One is thereby free of prejudice, and for that white person the race problem does not exist. It is assumed that if other whites would establish a similar relationship with other blacks on a one-to-one basis, then the problem would be solved.

Often the black person is unusual, a kind of superperson who achieved a great deal in the face of unusual odds. One is assured that if other blacks will so conduct themselves and meet acceptable standards, they too may be considered in the same way. Ironically, there is another way to acceptance, if one is able to play the role of a jester, or "clown." This is a short path to acceptance on an inferior level. It fulfills a stereotype and has the advantage of being easier and much faster.

What needs to be changed is not merely individual relationships; the entire social pattern of racism must be changed. It must be attacked on the individual and social fronts at the same time. It should not be necessary for a black person to be a superperson to be accepted as a person. If the so-called silent majority of whites, most of whom are average, have a right to the good life in this country, why cannot the ordinary person whose face is black be self-affirming and likewise enjoy the promises of America?

The reason why Black Theology is "political" is that the one-to-one approach is inadequate and unattractive to any black who is aware of the serious or insidious character of racism. Suppose a black person, however distinguished, strays from a social setting in which he or she is well known. Since prejudice is a prejudgment of the black person's inherent worth (and in view of his or her high visibility), it is not uncommon for very outstanding blacks to be mistreated in all parts of this country. Dr. King often referred to racism in America as a cancer whose malignancy had spread throughout the body politic. Since I speak of reconciliation, I would like to modify the figure somewhat because cancer is at present a terminal disease. But the figure of cancer does point to the seriousness of racism and the radical measures needed to eradicate it. Anyone who does not know how serious racism is, what it has done and what it is doing to blacks, is prepared to explain it away or approach it as a mild misdemeanor. No alarm or radical measures are seen as necessary. But the fact is that massive and radical changes are urgently indicated in the area of race.

Not only individual Christians but the church as an institution is condemned by racism. The genuine fellowship and fellow feeling of a few blacks and whites is important. But the churches as collective bodies, as structures of social, political, and financial power, are called forth to attack racism. Whitney Young speaks of the need for a domestic Marshall Plan to deal with socioeconomic problems resulting from the deprivations stemming from racism. It is not amiss to refer to a spiritual Marshall Plan in the area of race. This is what the Black Manifesto is about. But Christians must also call upon the resources of the nation — its wealth, power, and know-how — to right this wrong. Churches involved in empowerment and development programs among blacks must use their example, their moral influence, and their political strength to activate an entire nation to heal the wounds of an oppressed race.

Integration has been closely allied with the quest for civil rights, mainly through the courts. The enactment of laws was the basis for a hope that the promises of America to blacks would be kept. Beginning with the 1954 school desegregation decision, it was hoped that Americans would respect the law enough to grant blacks their rights. Endless litigation, and many political pressures, have caused black lawyers to lose faith in their own craft as the road to justice. Add to this the middle-of-the-road policy of President Richard Nixon, who has described the difference between *de jure* and *de facto* segregation so ambiguously that constitutional lawyers — even law professors and deans — were not sure what he intended. As if this is not enough, ponder the attempt of President Nixon to bring the Supreme Court under his control and through his appointments make out of it a conservative "constructionist" body of jurists who would be subject to an "advise and consent" relation to the White House. For all practical purposes, the balance of power in Washington would belong to the executive branch of government. We would have a "lame duck" judiciary in Washington that would merely rubber-stamp the Nixon program. With Vice-President Agnew as rhetorician, the future of the young, black, and poor American was hanging in the balance.

Kenneth Clark, a black social scientist who assisted black lawyers in writing the 1954 desegregation brief, argued that segregation has a negative effect upon black children. He then found himself a foe of the Nixon policy on desegregation. Clark said that the president "totally defaulted on leadership in achieving progress." Clark pointed out that the president's decision was political. The problem, on the other hand, was moral, ethical, and educational. He took away the momentum of the courts and the society.[6] Clark is a foe of separation — black and white.

Clark is now appealing to the enlightened self-interest of whites. He is saying that our society failed to take more than a token interest in doing away with segregated schooling and living. This way of living has inflicted insidious damage on privileged, middle-class, and working-class children. This country's inconsistency is in stressing democratic values while perpetuating undemocratic educational practices, thus helping to produce the rebellion against authority and against traditional values characteristic of the hippies, the drug cult, and the New Left.[7]

Clark is saying correctly that most whites have accommodated to the hypocrisy, rationalization, and prejudices of this society. But at the same time, there are increasing numbers of white youths who are rejecting all the values they see as favored by a hypocritical establishment that preaches democracy while it imposes the cruelty of racial segregation. From an educational point of view, it is imperative for whites to be exposed to blacks in the classroom just as much as it is for blacks to be exposed to whites. He points to the increasing instability of white youth as an indication that we have waited too long.[8] Clark concludes:

> Segregated schools are destroying the human development of sensitive white children more surely than that of black children.[9]

Whitney Young believes that this same self-interest is the only protection blacks have against suppression even in the form of concentration camps. He says:

> The reason they won't move in with fire power to shoot down blacks who are demanding their rights is that when they look through the sights of the gun and they get ready to corral the people to go to the concentration camps, they will find their own children.[10]

Both Clark and Young are distinguished and perceptive scholars and leaders, but they are somewhat misguided if they put that much trust in the enlightened self-interest of whites. A nation of people that will sacrifice its sons to the Moloch of war out of pride will willingly give up its sons and daughters for pride of race. Even white ministers have disowned their sons who got too deeply involved in racial understanding. Several of my closest friends have been thus disowned. A theological understanding of humans and the radical manner in which sin as pride can corrupt human nature and cause disorder in society would enable blacks to understand what we face in racism. It is a situation in which the finite has exalted race to the level of a God-substitute. A radical change—like a religious conversion, like death to sin, and resurrection to newness of life—is the only ultimate solution to the blight of segregation upon oppressor and oppressed.

Waldo Beach is correct, I believe. He says:

> The problem of race is at its deepest level not a factual problem, nor a moral problem, but a theological problem. Its locus is not finally in man's cultural environment, nor in his inadequate knowledge of racial information, nor yet in his moral inertia. These are satellite powers to the final demonic iniquity, man's inner perversity of will, his worship of the finite.[11]

Alvin Pitcher distinguishes between the old and new liberalism. He says the old liberalism stands in the way of progress. It insists that the fundamental principle of our society is equality of opportunity. But the new liberal believes in the equality of results. The old liberal believes in preparation, and preparation leads to participation, and participation leads to justice. The new liberal, on the other hand, believes that justice comes only with compensatory opportunity. Pitcher sees this in Black Power and black separation. Black Power is the new principle for organization, and black separation refers to black-owned and black-controlled institutions.[12]

Pitcher says it is easier to deal with bigots than it is with a mindset or self-assurance that continues to give old answers to new questions. He goes on to illustrate what he means by the new liberalism.[13] If children graduating from inner-city schools cannot read while those graduating from schools in the suburbs can, we have a racist situation. Wherever an institution can be said to demonstrate or to represent inequality of results, so far as black and white people are concerned, it is racist. Then he goes on to spell out what he means by special opportunity or compensatory opportunity. This is usually described by old liberals as discrimination in reverse, as un-American and as unconstitutional. This is an instance in which law may get in the way of justice.

Pitcher goes on to say that unless something extraordinary is done to improve the plight of blacks, equality of result will be a long time emerging—if ever. Since many people do not accept this principle, the only way to effect it is for those people who will benefit most from it to organize themselves to obtain equality of results. This is Black Power.[14] Pitcher says:

Equality of results will not come about until we can build some Black Power. If you begin to think about how we are going to get four times as much spent on the city schools as we now have spent, when the control of the money is in the hands of the people who are least willing to give up their power and to open their pocketbooks, just by going into their homes or into their business and persuading them, I think you are aware of the problem. So equality of results will not come without the power.[15]

And finally Pitcher speaks directly to the funding of power:

Of course if you find somebody who understands power then he is liable to use it, but until we become true liberals . . . namely, that we are willing to fund the sharing of power with those who are powerless, we can look forward in this country only to chaos and frustration and protest and disintegration.[16]

Pitcher is taking a bold position. He is advocating equality of results, compensatory opportunities, Black Power, a new sense of black community with dignity and respect.[17] Otherwise we take the risk of seeing our society pulled apart by a creed that is no longer adequate.[18] This is a revolutionary perspective, but it is close to the insights of Black Theology concerning liberation and reconciliation.

How do freedom and reconciliation hang together? As I observe what other black scholars in the field of religion are saying, they mean exactly what I mean by liberation. In bringing this chapter to a close I shall use their language. Joseph R. Washington, Jr., in spite of his many changes, holds on to the belief that the promotion of freedom has been the theme of black religion from its inception. The black church has had freedom as its goal—and still has. Any worthy Black Theology, according to Washington, must be a "theology of freedom." Freedom is the fundamental concern of all black people. Freedom is the "heart and whole of the black church."[19]

Freedom is the test of the quality of black existence. Without freedom black people will perish, and with them their neighbors. Freedom is the only salvation the black church has to offer, and freedom is the only hope of humankind. According to Washington, no one can be faithful to the Lord of history who does not take this theme of freedom seriously. The task of the black church and Black Theology is rethinking upon black religion as a religion of freedom. Black people must look again at what freedom has meant in their history and what it means in their present. Freedom, as the essence and unifying principle of black religion, must be illuminated by Black Theology.[20]

> It is only through searching into the history and meaning of black people in the light of freedom and bringing to bear this theology of critical thinking upon the present ... that a contribution is made to black people and thus to all people by the black church under the aegis of Black Power.[21]

Now Washington has been talking about "freedom" ever since he wrote his first book, *Black Religion*. What is different is that he now associates freedom with Black Power:

> An authentic Black Theology would begin with its response to God and to its fellowmen through an engagement in intellectual combat with Black Power as to the nature of the freedom pursued by all in behalf of all.[22]

In *Black Religion*, he presents a theology of freedom. In *The Politics of God*, he presents a theology of suffering. Black Christians become "chosen people" or "suffering servants." In *Black and White Power Subreption*, he develops the theme of revolutionary theology. In all cases "freedom," or what I have called "liberation," is the unifying thread. In his discussion upon the theme "Black Power Theology,"[23] Washington outlines the shape he views this new theology as taking. He does not do any significant theological construction. After assessing Washington, Cone, and all other black scholars working at the problem, I feel that the constructive phase of Black Theology is yet undone.

There is one instance at which Washington points an inquiry in the direction I am moving. After indicating what he views as a rapprochement between black church leaders and Black Power advocates, after establishing their mutual need and dependence upon each other and after lifting up what he sees as a futile, though an honest belief held by black Christians that they can force white power to move beyond tokenism, Washington speaks of reconciliation in black-white relations:

> Reconciliation in Black Power does not come on the other side of power; it comes on the other side of revolutions and redemption. Black Power is a demand for a theology of revolution that includes reconciliation after conflict, not just after separation ... Is there a Black theology of reconciliation growing out of revolution? ... At the heart of the Christian faith is redemption out of revolution and through reconciliation.[24]

There is no surety that Washington and I are together on means, but what I am setting forth here is in essence "redemption out of revolution and through reconciliation."

I would agree with Preson Williams in his critique of Washington's unusual stress on freedom. Williams wants to make the point that there have been times and circumstances in the black experience in which we knew that "freedom" was not possible. In these instances blacks made the necessary psychological and religious adjustments necessary for survival. In such instances what I have called the "search for meaning" rather than the "quest of freedom" was most characteristic of black religion. Every adult black living today can remember—not with pride, but as a fact—instances in which survival rather than freedom has been a choice. In such cases, meaning for existence in spite of oppression rather than freedom as an alternative to oppression has been accepted. Black Power militants call us "Toms." They say that they blame us and the religion that led us to make the wrong choice.

What they often forget is that in life we face not a theoretical but an existential situation in which life and death hang in the balance. It was to our credit that instead of hatred and revenge, our Christian faith enabled us to transmute suffering into many victories in our own lives and in the lives of other blacks and whites. What young black militants will soon realize is the wide chasm between rhetoric and reality, and that confronted by an existential situation, many are not yet ready to die. This is an observation made by a young black militant who said he had himself together.

Another student who was disenchanted with Black Power told of how he lost his personal freedom. Along with other militants he was caught in a building on his campus when the administration called in the police. He said the majority wanted out but the leaders would not let them out. They suffered, therefore, unwillingly, by association. Under such circumstances, many black militants have discovered the difference between being a camp follower and being committed to a politics of survival that may require willingness to surrender one's life. Thus I have spoken of meaning and protest, liberation and reconciliation in relation. A worthy Black Theology has to be balanced in this way.

In the fall of 1968, the Student-Faculty Committee on Racial Crisis at the Divinity School of the University of Chicago sponsored two distinguished black scholars in a discussion. Fortunately, the essence of the exchange between Charles Long in history of religion and Nathan Scott in theology and literature was published. Long, the younger scholar, expressed real understanding of the current black revolution in an essay entitled "The Black Reality: Toward a Theology of Freedom." In a conversation with Karl Barth on the American experience, he spoke of the need to develop in this country a "theology of freedom." Barth spoke of the United States as a strange place. In his *Evangelical Theology*, he refers to his encounter with Long as a "dusky theological colleague . . . a literally black colleague."[25]

Long picked up Barth's suggestion as a theme for discussion. Long sees the black community as presenting what he calls a "hermeneutical task" involving new and fundamental interpretations. "How are we to construe," he asks, "the terms 'life,' 'liberty,' and 'happiness' for non-Europeans?"[26] In pointing out that the black reality remains the central issue of American culture, he says:

> American culture has yet to come to terms with its "native sons"—
> and this is just another way of saying that America has yet to come
> to terms with itself. Religiously speaking, America must be afforded
> the religious possibility for the experience of the *mysterium tremendum*,
> that experience which establishes the otherness and mystery of
> the holy. It is this element of holiness that is so familiar in my background.[27]

Long had said at the outset that "my native land has always been for me a strange place."[28] The black community presents what he calls an other attitude:

> A reality so agonizing that it forced us to give up our innocence while
> at the same time it sustained us in humor, joy, and promise. I am
> speaking of a quality of the American experience which through its
> harsh discipline destroyed forever a naïve innocence, revealing a god
> of creation—a god of our silent tears—a god of our weary years. This

may be called "nitty-gritty" pragmatism. It is from this kind of history and involvement with nature, man, and God, that germinates the dense richness out of which profound religious awareness emerges.[29]

Long concludes with a note on reconciliation:

> The distance and otherness evoked by the racial situation might give both sides the possibility for a kind of humility — the humility to reflect on their common creaturehood, and, I may add, an invitation to participate in both the tragedy and comedy of human existence.[30]

Nathan Scott gave a worthy response to Long's paper. It is possible to observe a generation gap between these two black scholars. Scott has arrived at an unusual standing in his field of theology and literature, but his references to the racial crisis are notable by their absence.

Scott as a theological interpreter of art and culture could render an invaluable service to the cause of self-understanding and theological liberation. In an essay in honor of Richard Wright, Scott has described the racial situation as "the extreme situation" and spoken of a need to deal with the "black presence" in all artistic expressions.[31] He has not given his genius to a mature interpretation of the black religious experience. His silence is a tragic loss to black liberation as it is to any black-white reconciliation.

A colleague of Scott's at the Divinity School had spoken of the American religious experience in terms of "the logic of communion." Scott rightly retorts that this logic has often been rather "a logic of exclusion, at least of the darker brethren."[32] The religious enterprise in America has been greatly impoverished as a consequence of this exclusion. American religious experience has been implicated in duplicity and has suffered from insights and meanings due to the predominant indifference to black experience. Scott is an integrationist of the old school, and therefore he uses Negro instead of black as a reaction to Negro militants with a racist outlook. He does not want to preclude the black-white exchange of values that has actually occurred. But he does want to bring into focus that aspect of our heritage which awaits interpretation. In this same spirit, I had to reassure some black scholars recently that the purpose of an authentic Black Theology is to accentuate the positive aspects of our religious heritage, the interpretation of which has been omitted by theologians and church historians alike, that our program will be pro-black rather than anti-white.

In direct response to Long, Scott deals with what the former has referred to as the otherness of the black experience. Scott is existentialist in orientation. I would hazard a guess that his experiences as a black man together with an identity crisis (which is a problem for all black scholars) explain his fondness for existentialism. In the area of human relations, he is for Buber and against Sartre.

He reminds us that Christians must understand otherness in a manner that does not rule out reconciliation. Sartre, we are told, has presented an unacceptable view of "the other" in *Being and Nothingness*. Sartre has conceived the relation between persons in terms of conflict. To consider another is to reduce the other to an object and limit his freedom. When two persons look at each other, they become each other's slave. Sartre describes the interpersonal situation as one of threat, uneasiness, tension, and struggle. In *No Exit*, Sartre sums it all up by saying: "Hell—is others."

Scott sees in the Jewish philosopher Martin Buber the insight that persons become truly human only in their relations with one another. Real life is a "meeting." In the beginning is "relation." The I only begins deeply to enter into its own identity as it encounters the thou. Thus human existence is an affair of mutuality or dialogue. People need to confirm one another by means of genuine meetings. They need to see the truth of others, who are their brothers and sisters. The interhuman is a realm where reality is an affair of sharing, of free encounter, and where one comes into full possession of one's true stature.[33]

Accepting Buber's model as normative for otherness in the black-white relationship, Scott turns to Long's statement again:

> To learn how to live with otherness, as a nation confronts the new militancy of the Negro community . . . given the profound extent to which black men and white men have entered into a blood relationship, *la présence noir* will never be simply a sheer otherness. But otherness . . . no doubt there will be.[34]

Long had said that the American religious experience demands a theology of freedom. He had indicated that the black religious experience, having been carefully neglected, needs now to be consciously dealt with. He had described this black heritage as an extremely hermeneutical task. In conclusion, Scott raises this issue:

> Is "the other" to be thought of as enemy? Or, are black men and white men to think of themselves as each a part of the other?[35]

It is my view that Long and Scott are both right. The radicalism of Long and the maturity of Scott must merge in any worthy and lasting contribution. There can be no real reconciliation between blacks and whites henceforth without liberation. No white liberal or black moderate will be able to turn the clock back. As Dr. King put it: "No one can ride your back unless you stoop." Black youth desire to move into a future where one does not need to stoop because of black skin. We must be liberated—Christ is the liberator. But the liberating Christ is also the reconciling Christ. The one who liberates reconciles, and the one who reconciles liberates.

3

Search for Black Peoplehood

One needs to be aware of the perils as well as the promises of the idea of a chosen people. The concept has been more frequently exploited and misused than it has been properly and fruitfully used. The usage has often been deadly to an oppositional group, but it has likewise been negative in its effects upon the sponsoring group as well. Both positive and negative results of the concept of a chosen people may be found in the history of the Jews (the original chosen people). The religio-political usage of the concept by Germans and Japanese during World War II should give us pause. Hindsight should inform any black theologian who anxiously climbs upon the slippery slopes of this difficult concept. He or she must be cautioned to tread softly and slowly.

I have spoken of the perils and the promises of the concept. Both need to be explained further. However, my reason for examining the concept is explained by the fact that I believe the promises outweigh any difficulties. The difficulties need to be faced and isolated before one presses on to a constructive statement of the "chosen people" in relation to blacks.

One of the cardinal concerns of Black Theology is this "enigma wrapped in a mystery" and known as "the chosen people." James Baldwin often reminds us that blacks should not embrace myths that have made whites blind to their vulnerability—that is, belief in the manifest destiny of white America. If black people can be in any sense saviors of America, they may be to this extent a chosen people. They are in their "chosenness" messengers of grace—not merely ministers of death. I am aware that some blacks have elected themselves judges and executioners of whites for their evil deeds. For these prophets of hate, revenge and revolt have become their only creed. My understanding of the Christian faith leads me to reject this path.

In the study of Nat Turner's *Confessions* one discovers a religiously motivated but bloodthirsty path to "revenge and revolt." We need not rehearse here this ill-fated incident except to indicate that history need not repeat itself. But we are at the same time reminded of the Puritan revolution,

21

sometimes referred to by historians as the "revolution of the saints," as an indication that whites as well as blacks may misread and misuse their Bibles. It is said that Oliver Cromwell, Lord Protector of this mid-seventeenth-century English revolution, read the "warring books" of the Old Testament and knew God only as a God of wrath. The "steadfast love" of the God of Israel and the *agape* of the God of Jesus were unknown to him. Blacks, therefore, may likewise see what they desire to see in the Bible. It is the task of Black Theology to attempt a constructive statement of what it really means to be a "peculiar people, an elect nation—the chosen of God." This will require of black scholars a careful rereading of the Bible through Christian eyes.

Rabbi Richard L. Rubenstein has an interesting argument in his *After Auschwitz*.[1] He admits that Israel lost its "chosenness" for not fulfilling its divine mission. He "psychoanalyzes" Jewish history in the Christian West. His analysis is Freudian, and therefore he makes much of the sons slaying their father for the love of their mother. After the sons killed the father, they discovered that the father was more potent dead than alive in the amount of guilt emitted.

Against this belief background, Rubenstein recalls that the new Israel, the church, the new chosen people, has sought to replace the old Israel, the Jews from the time of Christ. Since Christ was God, Christ killers were accused of being guilty of deicide—they were considered murderers of God. This is surely an unpardonable sin, for which no amount of grace is sufficient for atonement. Thus, just as Freud's sons return again and again to the place of the deed, we return again and again through myth and ritual. For example, Catholics retrace their steps symbolically in the Mass. The death camps of the Germans in World War II, according to Rubenstein, may be explained in part by the anti-chosen people posture of the Germans. Being for Teutonic culture and against Latin culture, the Germany of Hitler was at once anti-Jewish and anti-Christian. The Christian church was far too well established to be attacked; therefore, the original chosen people, the Jews, were the scapegoats.

In the light of Christian scholarship, Rubenstein leaves much to be desired. But one does find this attempt to come to terms with the death camps and the birth of Israel exciting. After one reads Rubenstein's analysis of the tragedy of his people as a result of their "chosenness," one begins to wonder if blacks are not assuming yet another cross. As someone has well said, blacks should not be asked to take up yet another cross, having been burdened with one so long. This would be true if the Christian faith did not include cross-bearing for all Christians. This would be true if the cross were for Christians a symbol of defeat. But on the contrary, it is a symbol of victory. Black Theology must not attempt to take the cross out of the Christian faith. It must speak, rather, of how to pass through suffering, of which the cross is the chief symbol, to a larger and fuller life.

For some strange reason, the oppressed often think of themselves as the chosen of God. Perhaps this is basically an attempt to make some sense out of their oppression. It also helps to deal with the problem of Job—the problem of suffering in a world created and sustained by a God of moral integrity. If the oppressed can believe that their suffering as a people prepares them for a special mission in the world, some of the sting is taken out of their suffering. If black Christians are aware of the mistakes others have made in appropriating this concept, they may be able to use this concept in a helpful manner. The interpretation may be informed by the misunderstanding that Jesus and his followers have always held in focus concerning the failure of the Jews to understand fully and to carry out a proper mission as the chosen of God.

Many blacks are turned off by the idea that their suffering as a people may have some purpose. Even as a theologian who has searched for meaning in the concept of redemptive suffering, my emotions recoil at the idea of further suffering for blacks, even if that suffering may be fruitful in the end. Whenever someone makes the suggestion that perhaps the clue to the black chosenness is suffering, my mind raises real questions. The crucial question is representative. Is it necessary that such oppression and undeserved suffering continue in order that grace may abound? My suspicion is aroused further by the fact that the affirmative attitude toward human suffering comes from the side of the oppressor and not from the oppressed themselves. This leads me to suggest that whatever understanding of our chosenness emerges in a Black Theology, we must take into serious account the fact that the black experience has been purged in the fires of suffering. But our interpretation of chosenness must at the same time hold up the promise of a better day. The uses of our past must be for the redemption of our future.

Joseph Washington and Albert Cleage, though poles apart in most respects, raise once again the question of the chosen people in reference to the blacks. Since the people of the Old Testament are a favorite for black people, it is not too difficult to understand why this theme continues to occur in black religious thought. Israel of Deutero-Isaiah was a suffering servant of God, a remnant and a saving minority. Jesus was the "son of Man who suffered." It is not strange that blacks should understand their peoplehood and discipleship against this biblical imagery and history. Thus Washington says:

> As a result of this suffering by a whole people for four centuries and placed in the perspective of the Bible, we contend here that the Negro cannot be understood or understand himself except as another "chosen people."[2]

Cleage makes a similar claim:

> We believe in the doctrine of Black Power as a religious concept revealed to us, as God's chosen people, in the Old Testament and in the teachings of Jesus.[3]

Washington's statement has real possibilities. It deals with the perils as well as the promises of the concept of a chosen people. He has a firm stand within the Judeo-Christian tradition. His consideration of the Jews is limited to the Bible and even this is interpreted with a Christian bias. He does not raise a question regarding the long-suffering of the Jews at the hands of Christians and what this might mean for black people's understanding of the "suffering servant." It is to Washington's credit that he provides the historical and sociological context in which Black Theology must treat the symbolism of the suffering servant. The black experience of suffering is related to the biblical message of redemptive suffering. Black Theology must, I believe, move beyond this to a more comprehensive understanding of suffering in history down to the present. For example, the suffering of the Jews in the Nazi death camps and the suffering of blacks as slaves and second-class citizens must be compared. Jews have suffered since Christ, as well as before Christ. As those accused of deicide, they have suffered two millennia, and as a result of this suffering during their diaspora, they have developed a profound theology of suffering independent of the person and work of Christ. Black Theology will do well to profit from this significant tradition.

Washington leaves undeveloped the most important aspect of chosenness for Christians. He only hints at the role Jesus Christ played as the suffering servant. The role of the church as the new chosen people is ignored altogether, so far as I am able to determine. A complete version of a chosen people in a Christian understanding of black experience must include what the early Christians conceived their mission as a chosen people to be, to what extent they fulfilled this mission and to what extent they defaulted. It is my impression that Washington seized upon a crucial problem for Black Theology but did not take his insights into a constructive phase.

My dissatisfaction with Albert Cleage's position is much greater. But my first task is to present in essence what Cleage has to say on this subject. What Cleage has to say is woven into what he has to say on black nationalism in religious dress. Cleage intends to present a Christian position, but what he actually presents is what Vincent Harding correctly calls the "religion of Black Power."

According to Cleage, Jesus came to build a black nation. When Jesus picked the Twelve, this was the beginning of the black nation. Blacks who wish to belong to the black nation must think of what is best for the nation rather than of what is best for them as individuals.[4] Jesus is said to be the black messiah who came to build a black nation.[5] Since Jesus is a black messiah in a literal and historical sense, Cleage must trace his genealogy through the history of "black Jews." Through his study of biblical history, it becomes "black history." He expects us to reject all the intense critical-historical study of the Bible available and accept his restructuring of Bible history without benefit of any references.[6] It follows that he takes his collectivistic approach seriously. Such credulity should not be expected of even the most devout "soul mates." He says:

> Jesus was trying to rebuild the black nation Israel and to free it from Rome, the white oppressor. When we say the nation Israel, we are speaking of the black Jews of the Biblical period, many of whom still remain in Israel and the Arab world.[7]

We must take Cleage seriously, however much we may disagree with his understanding of the Bible, his theology, or his program. He somehow speaks to many blacks in a manner that few ministers do. He understands "the mood ebony" and he is deeply aware of the needs and frustrations of black people in the inner city as few ministers are. He gets an immediate visceral approval from blacks little given to sound reflection upon the tenets of the Christian faith. This group includes not only untutored blacks but also many young black intellectuals who have never been exposed to an academic study of any religion. Cleage makes immediate contact with black consciousness, black pride, and Black Power, and then goes on to present a religious nationalism that fulfills the spiritual strivings of black people. It is my view that Cleage contributes little to a worthy Christian understanding of what chosenness should mean in the black experience. But this attempt to Christianize the religion of Black Power must be dealt with.

I have already spoken to some points of weakness in Cleage's position. There are others, however, from my point of view. Cleage's position is exclusive in a strict sense, and this is true in a theological sense. His christology is wrapped up in a black messiah. His understanding of the church is bound up with the black nation. The aspect of a doctrine of sin that treats moral evil stemming from human estrangement is treated in the same exclusivistic manner. Sin is social or collective, but not personal. Love is to be operative only between soul brothers and sisters. It is the principle of unity and fellowship within the black nation, but it does not enfold the white person. Thus at the point where theology and ethics meet, Cleage faces a serious problem.

Without discussing, in this connection, the doctrine of sin as a whole, and without raising the issue of reconciliation between blacks and whites, Cleage holds a rather romantic position regarding the so-called black nation itself. Any group consists of persons-in-relation or individuals-in-community. There is always the self and the other self. Therefore, the psychology, as well as the sociology, of group life is to be considered. From the point of view of theological ethics, the "black nation," should it exist, would be not only sinned against; it would be a sinning community. Cleage has not provided realistic safeguards against the inevitable frictions and exploitation that would exist in any human group. Thus Cleage's chosen people, the black nation, has been launched upon a stormy sea where the ship is at the outset beset by the peril of exclusiveness, and the problems of mutiny upon the ship itself may lead to its utter destruction. The Christian understanding of humanity as sinful is a robust realism. But the Christian faith is optimistic about what God can do in and through our being open to others and to the agency of the divine spirit and grace.

Of the two black scholars, Washington and Cleage, whose views are representative, my choice would be Washington. It appears that he has raised some of the real issues to be developed in a theological interpretation of black people as chosen people. The black theologian has no license to ignore sound scholarship in interpreting the black experience. His or her task is to make creative use of all scholarship toward a better understanding of what the Christian faith can mean for a suffering people. Since his or her people present a prime example of a suffering people, a correct understanding of the message, meaning, and mission of suffering in their experience may enrich the Christian witness among all people — especially the oppressed.

The chosenness of black people is related to the entire concern of Black Theology. It is related in a special way to such concerns as the nature and character of God, the nature and destiny of humans, the person and work of Christ, the nature and mission of the church, and eschatology (realized and unrealized). The concept of a chosen people is important for the unity of purpose among black people and the feeling that their group life has lasting and salvific significance. But this "getting together" must not overlook the need of each black person "to get self together."

Some black students made a revealing discovery within their own group. They became aware of the need to have sensitivity sessions within their own ranks in order to relate to one another — not merely to react to whites out of a "psychology of oppression." They also discovered that the "cult of personality" had emerged in their group and that they desired to have the freedom of selfhood — to think and act for themselves, even with and for the group. They further discovered that they were too "ingrown," that they were "getting on one another's nerves," and that they needed to relate creatively and positively to persons outside the group for their own enrichment and fulfillment.[8] A deep understanding of "persons and communities" in the light of the Christian faith would have made all these possibilities plain. But in such cases, one listens to the young. One does not say, "I told you so," or "If you only understood the Christian faith." One is pleased that light has broken through and that real understanding has leaped over the generations!

A people chosen of God is a people who have entered into a new understanding of their mission in the world. Instead of being victims of suffering, such people transmute suffering into victory. It becomes a rod in their hands to enter into a redemptive mission among themselves and others. If they correctly understand the role of a suffering servant, they are not led to consider themselves as superior or favored people before God. They enter into a "stewardship of suffering" with the "wretched of the earth." Upon entering into a deeper understanding of how their own lives have been purged and purified by unmerited suffering, they become "a saving minority," instruments of God's salvific purpose for all humans. Only in this way may black people overcome the danger of assuming the posture of a chosen people and at the same time fulfill the promise and purpose of a "suffering servant of God."

But in keeping with our insistence that Black Theology speak of liberation as well as reconciliation, we must make the point that at the same time we use suffering creatively and redemptively, we must seek to render it unnecessary as a way of life. In the white racist society which is America, blacks have borne a constant cross for more than four centuries. All suffering has not, by any means, been an act of God; neither has it been redemptive suffering. Much that we have undergone has been a result of "human inhumanity" and does not arise out of a Christian understanding of God's providence. This is the cross of our experience that we must be rid of. At the same time, we seek to *transmute* suffering into victory; we must strive to *transcend* suffering that we as individuals and as a people may know the liberty of children of God *here* as well as *hereafter*. At the same time that we *seek reconciliation* through our role as suffering servants, we are to *seek liberation* from suffering stemming from being black in a white world. Once again our Christian faith as a search for the meaning of life and as a protest against unjust and inhuman treatment is justified.

The Black Church and the Black Family

When we consult the New Testament, we find several "images" of the church. The black theologian will be most interested in those images of the church that convey a sense of unity and especially the notion of peoplehood. Having been exploited by the principle of "divide and rule" by whites, blacks need a cohesive institution to overcome family disorganization and the social concomitant of the same. The black church, at once a religious and community organization, has real possibilities for fulfilling this primary need.

One of the most serious internal problems of blacks is family disintegration. It would be nearly impossible to find a group of people who have been able to survive great hardship without strong familial ties. The destruction of the black family has been deliberate during our sojourn in this country. Although the black survival is a miracle of grace, it appears that the black church, as "invisible" and as a visible institution, has nurtured this suffering race and kept it alive.

Martin Luther said to the German people: "If God is your Father, the church is your mother." The black theologian can correctly point to the black church as a family of God for those E. Franklin Frazier refers to as "homeless women and roving men." *Separation* of families during slavery was followed almost at once by the *scattering* of families during the migration to urban centers. This has been followed by a welfare system that almost finished off the possibility of a strong family system among blacks. The recovery of a meaningful family life for blacks is one of the greatest challenges facing the black church and its ministry to black people. The task may seem more hopeful if we remember that the black church was a family for blacks when there was no organized family.

One of the tragic things that white racist America has done to blacks is reflected in the splintering of the black family. It would be impossible for me, as a religious thinker, to surpass the research of Frazier, Billingsley, and other black sociologists who have studied the black family,[9] but their findings are to be seriously taken under consideration. The black theologian has the task of pointing up the role of religion in the history of the group life of blacks. Though Frazier treats both family and church in separate volumes, it is my observation that he did not connect family and church, and that he did not fully appreciate the importance of the black church as a home for the homeless and as a family for those without relation to or knowledge of their loved ones.

Many African tribes seemed to have a well-ordered family structure.[10] Billingsley describes African family life as follows:

> First, family life . . . united . . . two families with a network of extended kin who had considerable influence on the family, and considerable responsibility for its development and well-being. Marriage could neither be entered into nor abandoned without substantial community support. Secondly, marriage and family life in pre-European Africa . . . was enmeshed in centuries of tradition, ritual, customs, and law. . . . Thirdly, family life was highly articulated with the rest of society. The family was an economic and a religious unit . . . also a political unit. Family life . . . was strong and viable, and was the center of the African civilization.[11]

Billingsley's observation is representative of a real appreciation of a well-ordered family structure rooted in the African past of uprooted black slaves. The family system in Africa can be compared favorably with the celebrated Chinese family system. In both cases sociology and religion meet, for ties of familial kinship are associated with ancestor reverence. Family life in these civilizations formed a pattern of all human relations—physical and spiritual, secular and sacred.

Against this historical understanding of African family life, we begin to see the devastating and wrecking impact of slavery upon Afro-American family life. Males were taken away from their families in Africa. Families that came intact were splintered at public sales. In a document by Richard Clagett, March 5, 1833, entitled "Public Sale," one is reminded of what happened in Charleston, South Carolina, on that day. We read:

A valuable Negro woman, accustomed to all kinds of house work. Is a good plain cook, and excellent dairy maid, washes and irons. She has four children, one a girl about 13 years of age. Another 7, a boy about 5, and an infant 11 months old. 2 of the children will be sold with mother, the others separately, if it best suits the purchaser.[12]

Those like Moynihan, who refer to the black family as if it is destructive to the black community, should first consider what white racist America has done and is doing to the black family. The above sale of blacks as property, without regard to any human concerns, explains the beginning of the female-headed family and the disorganization of black family life. It is indeed a miracle that there remain so many strong black families, especially in the rural South, where slavery did its worst against black people.

Those who say: "Why can't the blacks do what the Jews have done?" should look at the history of slavery. They should also look at what "plantation and ghetto" have done to black family life within the last one hundred years. A large number of black people moved from a sharecropping situation (where they never got out of debt) to an asphalt jungle where their plight often grew worse. A Reformed rabbi recently reminded his congregation that family life was just as sacred as that in the synagogue. He implied that what the assembly of the faithful was in the synagogue in macrocosm, the getting together of the family was in microcosm. The essential unit of the familial and religious understanding of peoplehood has provided Jews with a type of psychological salvation that has carried them through much hardship.

This illustrates somewhat the possibilities of the black family and the black church in restoring unity and peoplehood to the black community. We can point to some strong families in the black community and we may do likewise in pointing to certain black churches as providing a real family for the homeless, the lonely, and the forsaken. It is now time to include the church as the family in our own self-understanding as a people of God. In this way, the role of the black church as a place of worship will be expanded to include social and political action as well. In this way the secular and the sacred will meet.

The "family" is one of the few "images" that still has rich potential for communicating meaning to black people. In spite of the history of family deterioration under a racist oppression, blacks still have romantic notions concerning an ideal family. This search for a wholesome family has deep roots in our Afro-American past. Therefore, the movement that is informed by black history, black consciousness, black pride, and Black Power will reinforce the place of family life in the black experience. It is exceedingly wise for the black theologian to make full use of this imagery in his or her Christian theological interpretation of the black experience.

Family life is universal; it answers to universal human requirements. It is a pragmatic way of satisfying and regulating the most fundamental needs of humans: the need for secure and predictable social companionship, for food, for sexual expression and regulation, for reproduction, and for the teaching and training of the young. The family is not only a social and economic institution—it is also a moral and religious school for children when it functions properly.[13]

The black church, as a social and religious body, has served as a kind of extended family for blacks. In a real sense, then, thousands of blacks who have never known real family life have discovered the meaning of real kinship in the black church. W.E.B. DuBois writes:

> The Negro church of to-day is the social centre of Negro life in the United States, and the most characteristic expression of African character.[14]

After describing the formal organizational and religious functions of the black church, DuBois adds:

> The [black] church often stands as a real conserver of morals, a strengthener of family life, and the final authority on what is good and right.[15]

It is meaningful to use the family imagery as we speak of the black church, for the family as it ought to be is characterized by a "relative permanence and ethical character."[16] Even though the human family has a physical foundation, it is primarily a moral institution.[17] The family, theologically speaking, is one of the "orders of creation." It is part of the established social order. It meets a need built into the divine creative plan for humans. In the beginning God decided that it was not good for man to be alone (Gen. 2:18). God, therefore, created woman and gave her to Adam as a wife (Gen. 2:24). To this union were born, immediately, two sons, Cain and Abel (Gen. 4:1–2). According to the biblical record, we are thus introduced to the first family of humans. The family has "in its essential nature a permanent and constituent element in human community life and embodies a definite mode of union among men."[18] Knudson concludes that "it is this definiteness, distinctiveness, and necessity of a social institution or mode of activity that constitute it as an order of creation."[19]

The family as a part of the divine ordering of human life meets the demands of sociability in group life in the most intimate manner possible. This aspect of human life is part of the universal experience of humans. This explains the presence of family life among all humans. The attempt on the part of whites to destroy this necessary bond between black men and women and their children illustrates the diabolical dimensions of our racist society. It explains why a recovery of this irreparable loss is so difficult. But the felt need for a realization of family life is present among black people as it is among all humans.

The black theologian has a great opportunity to make constructive use of "the family" as the people of God as expressed through the black church. Thus we speak of the beloved community, the black church, as the family of God. Here we refer to the church as it ought to be. If the black church is true to its nature and fulfills its mission, it can be for black people a family of God.

It is the image of family that best describes our peoplehood, that offers, I believe, the most constructive possibilities for a theological understanding of the church in general and the black church in particular. Paul, speaking to the church at Ephesus, says: "For this reason I bow my knees before the Father, from whom every family in heaven and on earth is named" (Eph. 3:14–15). Elsewhere he says: "So then, as we have opportunity, let us do good to all men, and especially to those who are of the household of faith" (Gal. 6:10). These words of Paul seem to be written especially for a homeless, hopeless, powerless people:

> So then you are no longer strangers and sojourners, but you are fellow citizens with the saints and members of the household of God, built upon the foundation of the apostles and prophets, Christ Jesus himself being the cornerstone, in whom the whole structure is joined together and grows into a holy temple in the Lord; in whom you also are built into it for a dwelling place of God in the Spirit. (Eph. 2:19–22)

The Christian church is a messianic church. It is a christological community. God is Father of the disciples because he is Father of Jesus. The disciples are to reproduce the activity of God: "You, therefore, must be perfect, as your heavenly Father is perfect" (Matt. 5:48). The Father confers the kingdom and the Holy Spirit on the disciples (Luke 12:32). Christians mediate God to others "that they may see your good works and give glory to your Father who is in heaven" (Matt. 5:16). And Christians owe their very spiritual existence to the Father—without him they could not live (Matt. chap. 6). Paul seizes upon Father as a distinctively Christian name for God, saying often "Blessed be the God and Father of our Lord Jesus Christ." In Ephesians (3:14f.) Paul speaks of "the Father, from whom every family in heaven and on earth is named." Paul insists that people are children of God, not by right but by adoption (Rom. 8:15, 23). Humans come to God as Father through Christ (Gal. 3:26). This sonship is a consequence of God's gift of the Spirit (Rom. 8:14). Paul expresses this essential dependence of the sonship of Christians upon the sonship of Jesus as follows: "He who had set me apart . . . was pleased to reveal his Son to me, in order that I might preach him among the Gentiles" (Gal. 1:15–16). The author of the Letter to the Hebrews speaks of Christ's self-identification with the believer. But the position is maintained that God's culminating revelation to us is in his Son:

But we see Jesus, who for a little while was made lower than the angels, crowned with glory and honor because of the suffering of death, so that by the grace of God he might taste death for every one. For it was fitting that he, for whom and by whom all things exist, in bringing many sons to glory, should make the pioneer of their salvation perfect through suffering. (Heb. 2:9–10)

Adelphos, "brother," is the universal, standard name for Christians. In the Old Testament, this meaning appears alongside "neighbor" and "kinsman" (Lev. 19:16–18). All refer to a member of the Hebrew community of kin. It means, first, the one with whom a man has common parents. Brotherhood corresponds with the idea of "family" (Gen. 24:4). The city community is a family and fellow citizens are brothers; therefore, all Israelites are brothers (Ex. 2:11). Brotherhood exists where there is "social unity" generally, but in some cases it exceeds these limits—for example, David and Jonathan (2 Sam. 1:26).

In the New Testament, *adelphos*, "brother," is used overwhelmingly in a Christian sense. Jesus said, "You have one teacher, and you are all brethren" (Matt. 23:8). But elsewhere he warns: "If you salute only your brethren, what more are you doing than others?" (Matt. 5:47). The implication here is that "family" in the Christian sense transcends the limits of blood relationship, because Jesus, "the desire of all nations," claims all persons as his brethren (Matt. 25:40). The status of a person is entirely changed by membership in the church. We are "no longer . . . a slave but more than a slave . . . a beloved brother" (Philemon 16).

The divine mission and the saving work of Christ point to such a fundamental unity with humans:

He who sanctifies and those who are sanctified have all one origin. That is why he is not ashamed to call them brethren. . . . He had to be made like his brethren in every respect, so that he might become a merciful and faithful priest in the service of God, to make expiation for the sins of the people. For because he himself has suffered and been tempted, he is able to help those who are tempted. Therefore, holy brethren, who share in a heavenly call, consider Jesus, the apostle and high priest of our confession. (Heb. 2:11, 17–3:1)

Jesus places great emphasis upon reconciliation in his use of "brother." Jesus puts it thus: "If you are offering your gift at the altar, and there remember that your brother has something against you, leave your gift there before the altar and go; first be reconciled to your brother, and then come and offer your gift" (Matt. 5:23–24). I John echoes this accepted standard of Christian virtue:

He who does not love his brother whom he has seen, cannot love God whom he has not seen . . . He who loves God should love his brother also. (I John 4:20–21)

Philadelphia, "brotherly love," remains an important aspect of Christian faith and practice. Even in Black Theology, liberation must never overshadow reconciliation.[20] The liberating Christ who is Head of the church, the family of God, is also the reconciling Christ. We are aware of the history of oppression. "Free indeed," as promised in the gospel, we understand to mean cultural, social, economic, political, as well as spiritual freedom. To arrive at this goal we may need to withdraw for a time from institutional expressions of racism, even within the visible church. Reconciliation in the church for black people must be beyond liberation from all types of bondage, and it must be reconciliation between equals. One may work for liberation as a prophet of hate and revenge, but one may work for reconciliation only as a prophet of love.

The black church must, nevertheless, proclaim a revolutionary gospel and live by a militant creed. The black church must be the church militant in the here and now. It must conceive of salvation in holistic terms. It must minister to all the basic needs of "black pilgrims in progress."

As those who have been part of a dispersion caused by slavery and subsequent oppression, we black people have known what it means to be "exiled," to be strangers and pilgrims. It would be natural for the black church to become the "pilgrim church," and thereby lead the white church toward its true nature and mission. To this end we may not merely be called but chosen—to show the churches that dare not risk the loss of funds, respectability, and social acceptance, how to be the church. The black church, which was "invisible" during slavery, and a haven for homeless, suffering people during all the years of our sojourn in white racist America, knows what it means "to sing the Lord's song in a strange land."

My understanding of the Christian faith leads me to speak of both liberation and reconciliation as proper goals for the Christian church in general and of the black church in particular. I understand the church to have a center but not a circumference—and exclusiveness to be a means to universalism and not its own end. Therefore, the black church, in setting black people free, may make freedom possible for white people as well. Whites are victimized as the sponsors of hate and prejudice which keeps racism alive. Therefore, they cannot know for themselves the freedom of Christians, for they are shackled by a self-imposed bondage. The cry for deliverance, for authentic freedom for existence, on the part of black people, may be salvific for all regardless of the nature or cause of oppression. The black church must address itself to internal strife and the sins of the oppressed. The black church must heal itself and overcome its own brokenness. It is a "sinning church"—though it is likewise sinned against. But the black church must be "healed" before it will be a healing church.

The black church in its suffering experience shares much with the earliest Christian fellowships. We have known the pangs of persecution, felt the lash of oppression, endured the fires of suffering, and yet we have persisted; we have truly overcome. The message of the Bible, the acts of God in the history of the people Israel, addressed the blacks existentially from the beginning. Even before we could read the Bible, the message of deliverance from bondage came through loud and clear. The so-called white Christians had fed to our black fathers and mothers opiate passages of obedience, servitude, and humility, but long before Nat Turner, the prophet of revenge, hate, and revolt, awakened whites to the incendiary possibilities of the Bible, blacks understood its message of "deliverance to the captives." Joseph Washington is correct. Freedom has been the mission and message of the black church throughout its history. What other group of Christians is in a better position to lead others as well as themselves into a vital understanding of what it means to be a suffering-servant people?

The essence of the Christian gospel goes right to the heart of the black experience. This is a good reason for the black church to become an agent of reconciliation. "God was in Christ reconciling the world to himself." Christians are called to be agents of reconciliation. We have every reason to hate, but we have been able to love and forgive. What but the grace and power of God can enable a mere human to rise to such heights? Reconciliation must be based upon a sound Christian understanding of God. Reconciliation must be based upon a proper appreciation of our dignity as those created in the image of God. While others speak of the nature and destiny of humans, the black theologian must first speak of the God-given dignity of humanity. This is necessary if we are to go on to a "moralized" understanding of reconciliation.

The assertion that all are "one in Christ Jesus" must henceforth mean that all slave-master, servant-boss, inferior-superior frames of reference between blacks and whites have been abolished. This principle must operate not merely on the spiritual level, but on the plane of human social relations as well. The slave must be set free, but the slave system must likewise be destroyed so that the future will be free of human bondage. The black church, as a family, as a corporate expression of the Christian faith of black people, is called forth into empowerment actions. It must become a *gestalt,* a structure of mass power of black people operating against oppression under Christian sponsorship. The black church must use all its resources to launch a massive assault against white power in church, community, or state that is responsible for the oppression of black people. But even in our revolutionary action for the liberation of black people, we must hold up at all times the possibility for black-white interracial fellowship and cooperation. Reconciliation between equals, no less than liberation, is the mission of the black church.

Religious nationalists, like Cleage, may reject the inclusiveness of the Christian family ideal. Black sociologists, like Billingsley, may reject the Euro-American concept of family life and exalt the African ideal. But if we are to speak as Christians, in a meaningful way, about peoplehood or family life, we must take the biblical message with all seriousness. Even if we ignore Paul and the later epistles of the New Testament and hark back to Jesus and the nation Israel, we still have a problem with the black family situation that needs urgent attention. Whether we seek to make black Jews or rediscover tribal Africa, the black family is still in trouble.

The family is a part of God's creative purpose. In all times (even from preliterate times) and in all known cultures, the family has been structured so as to meet human needs. The black family must also meet such needs. If we are honest, we must admit that many of these needs—for example, the needs of mothers for a lifetime companion, the needs of children (especially boys) for a deep relationship to a father—are not being met.

Although our first task is to become familiar with the root causes of broken family life, our efforts must not rest there. Neither may we afford the luxury of merely pinpointing the blame for the fragmented family life of blacks in white racism, as real as that has been and still is. As Christians we must do three things, at least. First, in our black churches, as free and powerful centers of worship and service, we must make of them an extended family. This must be done in order that black people who are lonely, homeless, powerless, and mistreated will find a real fulfillment of "soul" in the black church. Second, the black church, especially through its leadership, must use its power and influence to challenge White Power now being used to sustain a system that continues to cripple and destroy any meaningful family life among black people. And third, the black church must remind black people of their own sins and responsibilities. The black church that has a proper understanding of its mission can help to bring families together and inspire young blacks to go forth to establish stable families that will provide for the economic, emotional, moral, and spiritual growth of the young.

The black church, as also the universal church, is a visible fellowship, an institution, an organization with economic, social, and political influence. It is the only massive organization owned and controlled by black people in a white racist society. But it is, at the same time, an invisible fellowship, an organism of the Spirit. It is the household of faith, the family of God. In its nature and mission, it can minister to the whole person—to head, heart, and stomach. No other institution in the black community can make that statement!

It is important that we maintain this sense of togetherness, belongingness, human pride, self-respect, dignity, mutual love, and concern. What we call the family spirit must permeate the Christian fellowship of black people. Beyond this we must cultivate a black ecumenism that will establish a unity among black Christians as they affirm their peoplehood in Christ, which is denied them in white racist society. If we can heal the brokenness in family life, we shall be on the way to unity, power, and love among ourselves that will deal a powerful blow to structures of power that perpetuate the injustices against black people. The black church as a people of God, as the household of faith, as the family of God, must by word and deed uphold the ideal pattern of family life to young and old in the black community. In worship, service, and action, the "family" must be the model of all relationships both human and divine, to the end that the black family may be a part of the black church and the black church may be an extension of the black family, to the end that God may be "the Father, from whom every family in heaven and on earth is named."

4

The God of Black People

Prof. Herbert H. Farmer, whose lectures I heard at Cambridge University in the mid-1950s, has made an indelible impression upon all my theological thinking. His books, entitled *God and Men* and *The World and God*, are especially helpful at this point in our discussion.[1] In Christian theology the problem of God is related to the dignity and destiny of humans. So closely are God and humans tied together in theological reflection that it is almost a matter of indifference whether one begins reflection upon humans and moves to God, or whether one begins with God and moves to humanity. In the end, God and humans must be considered together in any worthy theological understanding of the Christian faith.

In this chapter I am attempting a succinct statement on God and humanity in the light of black awareness. A careful examination of what black religious thinkers have done on this subject is discouraging. In this century we are limited to Benjamin Mays's *The Negro's God* and other works, and to Martin Luther King, Jr., and George Kelsey on humanity.[2] Recent writers, such as Joseph R. Washington, Jr., and James H. Cone, have not yet grappled with this subject matter in any significant way. What I am able to do here is a mere beginning. The treatment of this body of material is overdue and is a significant part of any worthy Black Theology. Mays, Kelsey, and King wrote before the more recent trends in black awareness, pride, and power; therefore, their worthy contributions need to be reinterpreted, and the young scholars who are busy at theologizing need to reflect deeply upon the issues raised here.

Christianity is a "revealed" religion. It shares this status with several other world religions. This is a vital part of the Christian affirmation. Christians are not together on the sources, authority, and knowledge of revelation, but mere revelation, as such, is a part of the Christian's faith claim. Other religions of the same Semitic family, Judaism and Islam, accept revelation as a fact, though they differ concerning the medium and message of revelation. *God*, in Christian faith, is a revealer-God. God indulges in self-disclosure. God makes the divine mind, will, or purpose known to humans. Some Christians believe that this takes place through an infallible book (fundamentalist Protestants), through an infallible church through Christ's vicar on earth, the pope (Roman Catholic), through an infallible tradition expressed through the seven ecumenical councils (Eastern Orthodoxy), or through the incarnate Lord (neo-orthodox and neoliberal theologians—Protestant—namely, Emil Brunner and D. M. Baillie, respectively).

Karl Barth, I believe, is correct in starting his multi-volumed *Church Dogmatics* with a reflection upon God's self-revelation. Barth roots the doctrine of the trinity in the threefold revelation of God as Father, Son, and Spirit. This discussion of Barth upon the trinitarian revelation of God is his prolegomenon to his subsequent explication of the Christian creed.

The Judeo-Christian God, the God of the Bible, "unveils" through an "I-thou" encounter with the patriarchs, prophets, and people of promise in the Old Testament. God "fulfills" this same revelation in and through Jesus as the Christ. God continues to make Godself known through the apostles and the Christ. Through the agency of the Spirit, God within, the self-disclosure and unveiling of the mind and will of God is an experience of Christians in their personal lives.

Theology must deal seriously with the givenness of revealed truth. God speaks to the human condition. God speaks savingly to humans in a particular historical and cultural setting. Black Theology must, therefore, concern itself with the manner of God's address to blacks in the context of the black presence or the black experience of being a black person who seeks to confess faith in the God of the Christian creed, in black skin and in a racist society in which one is victimized. God's word is for humans. But what message does God give to black oppressed people here and now in the situation of racism?

It is to be expected that a God of wisdom and love for all humans will speak wisely and lovingly to each and every person—to each and every people. It follows that what God has to say to a person in the suburbs (affluent WASP, who enjoys the best of first-class citizenship in the most prosperous country in world history) will not be the same as that spoken to black victims of oppression whose main existential concerns are liberation—even survival—in a racist society bent not only upon segregation but upon repression. The person who is black, poor, unemployed (perhaps unemployable) needs a "word from the Lord." The revelation from God must be "strength and salvation" as one lingers in a rat-infested dwelling.

This by no means implies that someone in the suburbs with success and worldly goods is happy, or morally or spiritually fulfilled. There is too much evidence to the contrary. Too much has been written about "the split-level trap"[3]—even the "suburban captivity of the churches"—to believe such a fantasy. Indeed, many affluent white students have convinced me that their understanding of what God is saying is different from what their parents have understood.[4] I am making the point that when the human condition and the self-awareness that makes the difference known to the one who experiences it changes, then what God is revealing to humans is understood in a different light. What God unveils of the divine purpose to the slum dweller must be redemptive to such a person where that person is first, even if it also promises deliverance, as I believe it does.

The rationale for Black Theology is just this. Many of the best minds in this country, indeed in the West, have analyzed the needs of suburbanites who are white, Protestant, and prosperous. The sociotechnic interpretation of God's address to humans in the "secular city" has been ceaselessly examined. Black Theology must tackle the stubborn realities of "slum captivity" – of racism from the inside of victimization. The business of the black theologian is with the "other America" that is "black" – on the other side of the tracks, the other side of town, in the sharecropper's shack or in the dark ghetto. Blacks in good jobs, who live in clean neighborhoods, who are well traveled, cultured, and educated, are not free either, though some are pride-ridden and foolish enough to think so. In face of the reality of racism in America, the revelation of God to the black poor is equally valid, in most cases, to the black bourgeoisie. Once again this fact may be taught them by their own children. It is a fact, however, that those who are oppressed are most sensitive to the message of liberation. It is, for the black poor, good news. The revelation of God to blacks takes a particular form and carries a particular message.

Revelation, the address of God to blacks, is both personal and social. It is existential and political. It is concerned with earthly (material) things as well as with heavenly (spiritual) things. When God reveals Godself to persons, something happens in heaven, and something happens on earth. The physical-spiritual nature of revelation is consistent with the body-spirit nature of humans. Blacks must not make the same mistake as those who have been successful in the things of this world without God. Neither must religion be a mere opiate, an escapist ideology. God's revelation to blacks is at once meaningful for personal existence and a means toward the humanization of life.

God's revelation is a revelation to the whole person in all conditions and revelations. God's revelation reaches individuals in the depths of personal life. But God also speaks to the environmental conditions that make or break the human being who is made in God's image. God's address to the despised and rejected is aimed at restoring the dignity of those made in God's likeness. Revelation to blacks is a revelation of Black Power, which includes black awareness, black pride, black self-respect, and a desire to determine one's own destiny. Through God's revelation to blacks, the black person is enabled to transvaluate skin color into something comely and desirable, because a new self-understanding is now lifted up into the very creative purpose of God.

The making known by God through revelation of a creative purpose for human life and the sheer goodness of that creative act make it undoubtedly clear that black, too, is beautiful. The revelation of God as Creator, Redeemer, and Judge makes it abundantly evident that it is not given to anyone to rob another of a human birthright. Henceforth, one will be able to repeat with Jim Brown of "soul" fame (perhaps a strange prophet of the Black Revolution), "I am black, and I am proud." The black person, upon understanding God's address to the self, as black and poor, despised and rejected in a racist society, is assured that in the sight of God, one is somebody—"a child of God."

One of the great discoveries of Gautama Buddha, upon observing the caste system of Hindu society as sanctioned by the majority faith, was that one's spiritual condition rather than one's genealogy determines one's station in life. He declared that an untouchable (outcaste) who found refuge in the sangha (fellowship), who followed the four noble truths and walked the eightfold path, was a true brahmin (upper-caste Hindu). Gandhi endorsed this notion in calling the untouchables harijans (children of God) and by identifying his lifestyle, in many ways, with theirs. The mission and message of Jesus, the Word made flesh, the Chief Revealer of God to humans, are given to the common people, the disinherited, the oppressed. Thus the black person, reflecting upon the revelation of the God of the Bible and especially through the person and work of Christ, is convinced that through genuine Christian discipleship one is equal to every other member of the human race. God's revelation to the black person is a revelation of human dignity.

To sum up the meaning of revelation in the Christian faith, I want to make the point that theology, as reflection upon experience, must relate to what God is saying and doing to the human condition. God is a God who acts and takes action upon what is spoken. In this way revelation is related not only to creation and redemption but also to providence as well. All people are addressed by God as they are and where they are, even if they are called forth to change their place and condition. Before a personal or social revolution can be carried forth, God's word to humanity must be understood and appropriated. A worthy theological enterprise brings the revelation and the human situation together in order that a person may be able to find self or ethnic understanding, and thereafter liberation and fulfillment. This is the nature, medium, and message of God's revelation to humans, which is here applied in Christian theological perspective to black consciousness in a white racist society.

The question of the existence of God is not the real issue for blacks. This does not preclude the fact that many blacks are nonbelievers. This is often true of "cultured despisers" of Christianity, black intellectuals who equate their status with a militant rejection of the Christian faith. It is characteristic of many older black intellectuals who are humanistically oriented and are greatly influenced by the positivism of Auguste Comte. Add to this the lack of exposure to religious scholarship, the drive for money and success, which they believe will admit them to the mainstream, and the sentimental Jesusology of an ill-informed magico-religious upbringing, and one begins to understand why in their intellectual maturity, they have found their God "too small" and their religion inadequate. But the return to religion, often as blind faith in middle life, together with the spiritual strivings of their children, leads me to believe that religion is native to most blacks.

Religion in some form or other appears to be an Africanism that has survived all repressions that blacks endured in a white-oriented culture. Thus, I am taking the position that the problem of God presents itself to blacks in terms, not of the existence of God, but rather in terms of the moral attributes of God. Reflection upon the black person's God must deal with creation, providence, power, love, justice, evil, and the like. The Christian understanding of God must develop out of the black presence in a white racist society, and out of an experience of oppression endured for almost four centuries.

Black Theology affirms the goodness of creation. God is the Creator-Spirit. "In the beginning God created the heavens and the earth" (Gen. 1:1). And the creation is good—"and God saw that it was good" (Gen. 1:18). Humans were created by God as the crown of God's creative act. Then God said, "Let us make man in our image, after our likeness" (Gen. 1:26). Creation of nature and of human life is good. Whereas the affirmation of creation as good sharpens the question of evil in a world where creation is declared good by a God who is all-goodness and all-power, it also says yes to this life and all the material goods and services that make life worth living. If William Temple could look at nature through the eye of faith in the incarnation and declare that Christianity is the most materialistic of all religions, surely black people, who have been denied material things needed for a meaningful existence here and now in the name of this same incarnate Lord, need to reaffirm the goodness of creation as it comes from the hand of God, the Creator-Spirit. God, the Author of Nature, is the Giver of Life. All humans bear God's image, which is the sign and seal of their birthright—their personhood, their dignity. To affirm creation as good is to affirm the personhood of all human beings, including blacks, as a reality rooted in God's creative purpose and sealed by that creative act.

To affirm the goodness of creation is to accept, as correlative affirmation, the belief that the human person is a co-creator with God in the act of creation. When science is understood in this manner, it will be used as a means to make human life more human rather than as an instrumental evil seeking to be amoral or indifferent to human values. The affirmative attitude toward creation and human agency as co-creator with God is the basis for any worthy ecological understanding of the Christian faith. Human cooperation with God, in the procreative act, must also be viewed in all seriousness as a positive and purposeful act. God as Giver of Life acts through the human agency of parenthood to create human life, to sustain it, and prepare it for a worthy existence in the world. The Christian faith, therefore, combines "planned parenthood" and "responsible parenthood" through its affirmative attitude toward creation as good and humans as co-creators with God.

The need to affirm the goodness of creation is so strong that some black religious groups have done this at the expense of rejecting a doctrine of last things altogether. "The pie in the sky," futuristic hope of heaven, has been totally abandoned in favor of a this-worldly, realized eschatology. If I understand the Black Muslims fully on this point, they represent this type of reaction. If there be an objection that the Black Muslims are not "Christian," but Muslim, my reply would be that they do not belong to classic Islam either. This sect, in spite of its borrowings from Islam, is more of a Christian heresy than it is a genuine sect of worldwide Islam. Furthermore, many of the same "marks of oppression" that have given birth to Black Theology gave rise to the Black Muslims also.

My understanding is that a deeper understanding of "life everlasting" enriches and increases the meaning and importance of this present life. To see our present material existence from the vantage point of eternity gives greater urgency for the "holistic" realization of the best that this life can afford. Thus, an affirmative doctrine of creation holds the present and the future, the material and the spiritual, in a wholesome balance. The Creator-Spirit is Lord of History and the God of the Consummation. God as Alpha and Omega is also a benevolent-provident God. The Creator is likewise Redeemer and Judge. Some such interpretation of God as Creator, humans as co-creators with God, and the goodness of creation can speak words of comfort and hope to black Christians.

Over against others who speak so much about the absence and silence of God, it is a miracle of grace that black people have always had so much to say about the presence of God. Process theologians have, together with the "death of God" theologians, shared in the loss of transcendence in reference to the divine nature. For many Christians the "skies are empty." The biblical God, who is transcendent and immanent at the same time, is absent or silent. This understanding of God, which is "foolishness to the Greeks," but to black Christians "power and wisdom," still holds the field. The main reason, I believe, why this paradox has been unquestioned is that it is a sheer necessity for the faith of blacks that the presence of God together with divine activity for the realization of justice and equality in human affairs is clearly seen. For those who have come of age and can rejoice in their own strength apart from divine agency, this God professed by faith, who reveals Godself as near and far, as absolute and related, may not be so emphatically demanded. Even the God who performs miracles, the God of the gaps, is not expendable by the black and the oppressed in a white racist society. Almost daily, things happen in the experience of black Christians that cause them to burst forth in thanksgiving: "Thank God!" Suffering and tragedy often give rise to the expression "Lord have mercy!"

Blacks, in order to believe, are sustained by the presence and action of a God who is at once benevolent and provident. It is important that God be transcendent, that the divine be the ultimate standard of truth, holiness, love, goodness, wisdom. A God relative in these superb moral attributes would be a matter of indifference to a people victimized by hypocritical "pale copies" of these attributes among so-called white Christians and churchgoers. The black Christian has to believe in the existence of the best, that is, God the Father of Jesus as the Christ, through whom God reveals the divine self in flesh as "the way, and the truth, and the life."

Since Black Theology is addressed to a powerless people, a people seeking Black Power as a means of liberation from the oppressive control of White Power, the question concerning the omnipotence of God is of crucial importance. Some religious thinkers are prepared to sacrifice some of God's power to allow for infinite goodness. The conception of an impotent God is not very appealing to a people seeking Black Power for determining their own destiny. What is needed to inspire faith in the oppressed under the sustained domination of the oppressor is belief in a God of all-power who is able to promise the ultimate vindication of the good and the defeat of evil and injustices. The God of the Bible, the God of Jesus, is such a God.

In West Africa, the "high God" was a creator-spirit, but also a deistic god. This god was far removed from the experiences of the tribe. The high God was not lacking in power, but was otiose and transcendent. This god was, for the most part, indifferent concerning the events that transpired daily in the life of the villagers. The high God lived in the sky, for the most part, disinterested and passionless regarding the earthly plight of worshipers. Africans and Afro-Americans are deeply religious people. In Africa, religion is associated with nature worship and ancestor worship. Africans lived in a pool of divinity. It is not surprising that idols and incarnations of lesser spirits filled the void created by the absent god. The black slave, lonely, forsaken, without family, rejected, abused, and totally disinherited in a strange land, needed a divine friend. Possessing "an oriental mind," the biblical God met this felt need. The biblical record affirms, at once, the distance and nearness of God. The God of the Bible possesses all the exalted attributes of the African "high God," but, in addition, the biblical God is "closer than breathing and nearer than hands or feet." The God of the Bible is creator. This God is also a provident God who is savingly present. The God of the exodus, the God of the exile, the God of the prophets of social justice, the God of Jesus had a special appeal to this people of bondage. God is not merely present, but is present in power. The black preacher has found the Book of Daniel extremely attractive. Even if God wills to act contrary to the human will, as in the case of Shadrach, Meshach, and Abednego of the Book of Daniel, the moral honesty and ability of God are not questioned. This is the confidence blacks have placed in the God of the Bible. This faith has nurtured and sustained black people.

It has brought meaning to their hopeless existence and has been a means to physical and psychological survival.

The passage following is a reaction on the part of the three Hebrew children mentioned above to Nebuchadnezzar's threat to cast them into the fiery furnace. It comes close to the faith and understanding of God that has carried black people through the fires of oppression:

> If it be so, our God whom we serve is able to deliver us from the burning fiery furnace; and he will deliver us out of your hand, O king. But if not, be it known to you, O king, that we will not serve your gods or worship the golden image which you have set up. (Dan. 3:17–18)

All-power is a precious attribute of God for black people; for them impotent goodness has little appeal. Faith has to appeal, as Pascal has taught us, to "the reasons of the heart" as well as to "the reasons of the head." I submit that a God who is absolute in both power and goodness makes sense to blacks. Absolute goodness is important as well as absolute power. Absolute power ensures the ultimate triumph of the good; but absolute goodness assures us that absolute power will not be abused. While goodness is an intrinsic value, power is an instrumental value. God is manifest in what H. H. Farmer calls the "godness" of God. Power is the means whereby this godness at its best is manifest in human life and history.

God is love, love is God. Some argue that the difference between love in God and love in the best of humans is not merely a difference of degree, but a difference of kind also. But if we are to speak meaningfully of an attribute of God, there must be some analogical approximation with our own experience. Without this the "infinite qualitative distinction" of Kierkegaard holds. Only a blind leap of faith remains. I hold with D. M. Baillie that even the paradoxes of faith contain some analogy that makes contact with our humanity at its highest and best expression. The love of God is indeed a "love divine, all loves excelling," but we have "an earnest" of that love manifest in the best people we have known. Though it has always been imperfectly expressed, we have somehow recognized it, and the best in our own nature has responded to it.

It is easier to describe what love does than it is to define what it means. It heals the brokenness between persons, it overcomes estrangement, and it brings people together—it reconciles. Love is compassion. Love is redemptive. Love contains self-respect. It gives one a real appreciation for the dignity of others. God is love; love is God. The "inexpressible" gift of God for the reconciliation of sinful persons to Godself is evidence of the boundless measure of the love of God. God's saving grace comes to us in the form of self-giving love. It is nearly impossible to express the meaning of such love to an unloved and unwanted people. It is a "holing" experience to be the recipient of such love.

But love is often crucified. The fact that the cross is the supreme symbol of the Christian faith is a sobering fact to ponder. Sinful persons loathe to tolerate the presence of love. Black people have borne too many crosses to hold any romantic notions concerning the risk of love. Suffering and rejection have been their lot. Correlative with love as an attribute of God, there is the righteousness or the justice of God. One finds oneself in a "political" situation where the "pushing and shoving of justice" is a prerequisite for the expression of love. God is not only a Creator-Spirit, a loving Father; God is Lord of History as well. As a provident God, the divine has deposited a controlling purpose in history that promises to be fulfilled. By "justice" I do not mean to imply "equality"—the sense that blacks are expected to fulfill certain standards set up by white power in order to be admitted to the mainstream controlled by white people. Justice, then, in the sense of equity, implies a "God-given" right of the black person to expect dignified acceptance as a person "with all the rights and privileges of other persons."

In 1938 Benjamin E. Mays, now president emeritus of Morehouse College, wrote an extremely important book entitled the *The Negro's God as Reflected in His Literature*. To my knowledge Mays's book has no second before or since. It is not surprising that it has been reprinted as a part of the black literary renaissance. As literature it is one among many works, but as a theological document, it is invaluable. Mays wrote as a sociologist, psychologist, literary critic, historian, and theologian. He treated two basic types of black literature: "mass" or "popular," and "classical." In the former category he included spirituals, sermons, prayers, and Sunday school materials. In the later category he examined poetry, essays, and fiction.

Mays found two different conceptions of God reflected in black literature prior to World War I. On the one hand, there was a God of the masses, who would help eventually those who trusted and believed in the Divine Reality, rewarding them in the afterlife. On the other hand, there was the God of "classical" black literature, who created blacks in the divine image, and has elected blacks as in some sense "chosen." The former is other-worldly oriented, while the latter is this-worldly directed. The God of mass literature will deliver individuals from disease, sickness, hell, and enemies. The God of classic literature plays a larger role in bringing economic security to blacks here and now. After World War I, a third outlook emerged. There is skepticism about God. There is a threat to abandon totally the idea that God is useful as an instrument in perfecting social change. Doubt, frustration, protests, cynicism, and sometimes atheism characterized this trend. Many in Mays's own generation—many of his peers—took this route. E. Franklin Frazier and many of his associates at Howard University were among them. What is needed is an examination of what has happened in black literature since 1938 concerning the problem of God.

I see a development on two fronts: on the one hand, there is the religion of Black Power; and on the other hand, there is theological reflection upon

Afro-American Christianity–Black Theology. These present manifestations have been in the making for some time. Vincent Harding writes:

> Most of the authors and preachers who would be examined in such a work were only coming into life when Mays published his book. Jimmy Baldwin was beginning to shout in church; LeRoi Jones had not yet learned how to shout—anywhere. Malcolm Little was hung between Garvey's black Jesus and the blonde white hope of the American mainstream churches. Young Adam Clayton Powell was already preaching and marching in Harlem, but Martin Luther King Jr., was still sitting and listening and growing to the peculiar rhythms of Ebe-- nezer Baptist Church. Meanwhile, on the edges, in between the new and the old offering their own visions of interim Gods, were Richard Wright, Ann Perry, Ralph Ellison and scores of other anguished seekers.[5]

Mays finds, however, that the stereotyped idea of black religion as an opiate—as totally otherworldly—does not stand up to careful scrutiny. Protest and the faith in a God of righteousness and social justice is sometimes latent, but at others it is a creed for action. Mays, in describing the antebellum sermons of black preachers, wrote:

> It is conceivable that the literature of the period would be laden with other-worldliness and ideas of God that serve as an opiate to deaden one's sensitivity to slavery and other social problems. As strange as it may seem this is not the case. The Negro ministers of [that] period were keenly aware of social questions and they used God to support their claim that social righteousness shall be established.[6]

It is unfair to claim that such a God was a mental invention, "a wish fulfillment" born of psychological necessity. This is in fact the God of the Bible. This God is the Father of our Lord and savior Jesus Christ. This is the God of Moses, the God of the prophets, the God of Jesus—in a word, the Christians' God. The God of Christians is lovingly just. Any other God is inadequate and too small for the fulfillment of the Christian life. The Redeemer is also judge. God is love; love is God. God is just, and God establishes justice on earth. In the Christian understanding of God, love is not antithetical to justice. In the very nature of God, love is strengthened by righteousness and justice is tempered by mercy. God is lovingly just.

The experience of evil in a world created and guided by a God all-good and all-powerful poses a serious problem for Christian theology. If we are able to limit in our understanding of God one or the other, then we may place the responsibility for the existence of evil elsewhere. If God is limited in goodness, one may explain evil by this imperfection. If one can conceive of a finite God, then evil may be explained by an opposing will. Black

Theology, which is reflection upon the experience of being black and Christian in a white racist society, must hold to the all-goodness and all-power of God, as we have seen, out of sheer necessity. Furthermore, it is consistent with our understanding of the revelation of God. In the face of such a rational problem, one might immediately suggest a blind leap of faith. This might well be the "religious" solution, but theology requires "reflection" upon experience.

It takes little effort for a black person, conscious of the black experience of oppression in this country, to appreciate the problem of Job. It is not surprising that black preachers have preached so often and so meaningfully to their people from the Book of Job. Questions of black existence are raised profoundly in this book. This is not the only place in the Bible where these issues are raised. Habakkuk writes:

> O Lord, how long shall I cry for help, and thou wilt not hear? Or cry to thee "Violence!" and thou wilt not save? Why dost thou make me see wrongs and look upon trouble? Destruction and violence are before me; strife and contention arise. So the law is slacked and justice never goes forth. For the wicked surround the righteous, so justice goes forth perverted. (Hab. 1:1–4)

There are many examples of this cry of desperation in the face of violence and suffering in the Bible. Even from his cross, our Lord cries: "My God, my God, why hast thou forsaken me?" This is a very human cry, but such anguish is omnipresent to black people. Questions concerning the suffering of good people and the prosperity of evil persons, undeserved suffering, and related questions are commonplace to black people. I recently heard a black woman say, "I have given my life to God and I promise to serve him even if it hurts." At this time we were returning from the hospital where her youngest son lay seriously ill. But this same black Christian could appreciate fully the beauties of God's creation. I had heard her say to my wife, as we drove out in the countryside in the autumn when the forest gleamed in multicolored splendor, "God did a wonderful job on that tree." When she beheld a large tree that stood out among numerous other trees for its beauty, God became for her the divine artist. Here is a black woman of mature years, with limited education, but with a profound faith that has brought her through "many dangers, toils, and snares." It is a faith that appreciates God as the Creator-Spirit. But at the same time it is a faith in the God of suffering love—"a faith that will not shrink though pressed by many a foe."

Job was said to be a good man—a man of perfect moral uprightness. God had placed approval upon Job's life. All of a sudden Job loses all his possessions, including his children. His wife, who was spared apparently only to torture him, suggested that he "curse God and die." His friends, who came to mourn his loss and comfort him, offered their advice. It was the general belief on the part of his friends that Job was "reaping what he had sowed." There had to be a cause-effect relation between evil and suffering. Here was an attempt to make Job's suffering understandable, establish the cause for it, and exonerate God from any responsibility in the matter. God as Judge, as the punisher of the evildoer, had every right to mete out justice in such cases. But the drama of Job goes to great length to make the point that Job is a righteous man, that his extreme suffering was undeserved, and that any explanation of it is beyond human understanding. The happy ending of the drama of Job seems to anticipate Hollywood, though the tragic deaths of many of Hollywood's most glamorous stars give a lie to this theme in real life. Tragic endings in the theater of the absurd in the West and Japanese drama in the East are closer to real life. But it is the theological solution provided for the problem of Job, which has inspired the black preacher and the black Christian.

Job, slavery, and suffering caused by the oppression of black people are variations on the same theme—suffering, undeserved suffering, in a world in which a God of all-love and all-power is Creator, Redeemer, and Judge. If God is creator of everything, if God created the world *ex nihilo*, perceived that what was created as being good, where did evil come from? Even if we accept the existence of evil as an unexplained fact and decide that we must live with it, then why does God not put an end to it? Why does God as just, as all-powerful, as a benevolent and provident God, appear to allow evil to persist? It would appear that God's goodness would make evil intolerable and that the divine ability in the form of power would lead to the demise of evil. And yet the struggle against evil continues "and appears to be a real fight."

The negative approach of saying that those who do not believe in a God like ours have the problem of explaining the good, may be comforting but not very helpful. The solution that insists that all suffering is caused by sins must face the fact that the outright wicked person gets along so well in this life. The solution centering around the fact that suffering is a form of chastisement runs into trouble when one notes that often the best people we know endure too much suffering, while those who really need such chastisement seem to escape altogether. Why such an unequal distribution when the one said to be in charge is not only all-loving but all-wise as well? This is complicated when one takes up the experiences of blacks as a suffering race by the fact that some of the best people we know are black and some of the worst are white. The reverse is also the case, but the problem as to why all black people should suffer as they do remains. To say that evil is a partial good, that it appears to be a problem only because of our imperfect understanding, that if we could see experience whole and see it from God's perspective, the problem would not exist, does not stand up either.

I have made the point repeatedly that blacks are no better and no worse than whites; therefore, any explanation that does not make understandable the unequal distribution of suffering in the black experience is not helpful to black people. To point to the "thingness" of nature—that is, to the fact that humans live in two worlds at the same time, and that what happens to us as physical beings has nothing to do with our moral or spiritual condition—does explain some physical pain. We know that people who abuse themselves in their youth, morally and physically, may suffer for the same in later life regardless of a conversion experience leading to a devout Christian life. We know also that many misuses of the natural order leading to natural evils are related to moral evils perpetrated by persons of greed. This is what Earth Day and the emerging ecological theology are all about. But the why for slavery, for the widespread suffering of people in black skin simply because they are black and the inability to overcome this unmerited suffering more than one hundred years after the Emancipation Proclamation, remains "an enigma within a mystery" for black people.

It is little wonder, then, that Job's answer of a childlike faith makes so much sense to our suffering race. Job's words are our own:

Behold, I cry out "Violence!" but I am not answered; I call aloud, but there is no justice. He has walled up my way, so that I cannot pass, and he has set darkness upon my paths. He has stripped from me my glory, and taken the crown from my head. (Job 19:7–9)

In spite of all, Job confesses: "I know that my Redeemer lives" (Job 19:25). He will trust God even if God takes his life. The God who gives can also take away. The answer for Job is that God's will transcends human comprehension:

But where shall wisdom be found? And where is the place of understanding? Man does not know the way to it, and it is not found in the land of the living. (Job 28:12–13)

But according to Job:

God understands the way to it, and he knows its place. For he looks to the ends of the earth, and sees everything under the heavens. When he gave to the wind its weight, and meted out the waters by measure . . . And he said to man, "Behold, the fear of the Lord, that is wisdom; and to depart from evil is understanding." (Job 28:23–25,28)

This childlike faith is about as close as we get to an answer in the Old Testament to the experience of suffering. To go beyond this in the Christian understanding one would need to go into the cross-resurrection event. This is done elsewhere. What we have attempted to show is a biblical basis for absorbing the experience of suffering into a faith in a God who is Creator, Redeemer, and Judge. This faith is childlike, but it is not immature or childish. It is mature; it has endured much suffering and it has been the means to personal and social salvation of a long-suffering people. Some blacks have been embittered by suffering, like Nat Turner; others have been mellowed by it, like Martin Luther King, Jr. In all cases, suffering has accompanied the experience of being black in a white racist society. The Christian faith, through its doctrine of God as Creator, Redeemer, and Judge, has been a powerful assurance for black people.

The God of Moses, the God of the exodus, has been revealed to black people. This God is one of deliverance from bondage. The God who assures the Israelites constantly, "as I was with Moses, even so I will be with thee," has comforted, strengthened, and brought great assurance to black Christians throughout all their years of oppression in this country. Thus the God of the exodus is the black Christian's God.

5

Humanity, Sin, and Forgiveness

The experience of too many black persons, including the author of this volume, indicates that in the opinion of large numbers of white people in this country, the black person is not a human being. This includes not only the raging "racists" ready to destroy any black individual who gets in their way, but also many who are friendly to blacks, but who think of them only in an inferior frame of reference.

Black Is Beautiful: On Human Dignity

Before we can say anything in Black Theology about nature and destiny, we must affirm the dignity of the black person as a human being.

"Slave mentality" has controlled American race relations through the coexistence of blacks and whites in this society. The Dred Scott decision made the point that "the Negro has no rights that a white man is bound to respect," while stating that the basis for this is the fact that "he is not a citizen." The tragic underlying assumption is that one is not a citizen because one is not recognized as a person.[1] The black person is a thing, chattel or property, an object. There can only be what Martin Buber calls a "dialogue" or a "meeting," an "I-thou" encounter between subject and subject, not between a subject and an object. Insofar as this type of slave mentality prevails, there can be no real reconciliation between blacks and whites in this country. Black Theology is to enable black people to affirm their personhood, their dignified nature, which is God-given, and is not given or taken away by any human, black or white.

Benjamin Mays is concerned with an issue that must likewise be considered in a Black Theology interested in reconciliation as well as liberation in a society in which blacks and whites must find a way to coexistence. He is concerned with what discrimination does to the one who practices it. Hate destroys the hater as much as it does the hated.[2] A good reason for not becoming a black racist is to observe what discrimination has done to the souls, minds, and spirits of whites who hate blacks. To hate someone at sight, without ever getting to know another as a person, is a form of sickness.

Hate is a form of attachment. To really hate, one has to be dedicated. Keeping blacks down becomes a mission, a way of life. It is self-defeating and self-destructive. Segregation deadens the conscience and renders it untrustworthy as a moral guide. It makes white persons insensitive to pain, even torture inflicted upon blacks. Collectively, it enables total communities, including churchgoers, to turn away from moral evils, even murder, as long as blacks are the ones being victimized. Such insensitivity to human dignity of those created in black skin by a common Creator cannot be productive of making moral or spiritual giants.[3]

Mays seeks to recover the humanity of blacks. He does not wish to make second-class citizens out of whites. He argues that if whites will recognize the dignity of blacks, they will be surprised to discover that they have found their own humanity. Thus, he applies Christian principles in his understanding of humanity and appeals to the enlightened self-interest of whites at the same time. Many blacks, including many devout lay Christians, ministers, even theologians, have given up on both these points. The credibility gap is so great, based upon loss of faith in whites to do anything decent toward the recovery of true humanity for blacks, that these blacks seek only liberation for blacks "by any means necessary."

While the present writer shares much of the despair of the current impasse in black-white relations, he desires to make the point that humankind is wrapped up in a single garment of destiny, and for this pragmatic reason, if for no other, reconciliation between equals as well as liberation must ever be a goal. But, theologically speaking, we must make the point that the gospel is a reconciling gospel as well as a liberating gospel. Christian anthropology must take both seriously into account.

George Kelsey sees racism as destructive of human personality and addresses himself directly to whites who, because of its hold upon them, are not capable of living the new life of love—the Christian life is one in which "the pride of racism is overcome by faith." Hatred, fear, anxiety, hostility, insecurity, and self-glory are said to be the characteristics of racism. The life of the racist is a sinful, self-centered life. This self must be "shattered" and "destroyed" before it can be renewed. Racism is the purest form of self-glory; it exalts human beings over human beings. "Christian self-affirmation" is the solution to racism. It differs from all humanistic forms of self-realization, which promise self-fulfillment through striving. To affirm ourselves correctly, according to Kelsey, is to affirm ourselves in accordance with the divine purpose. Self-affirmation is the dedication of ourselves to God; it is not striving.[4] And "true self-negation means to be 'crucified with Christ.' Thus, the selfish ego dies. The 'I' turns away from itself to the 'Thou.' "[5]

Kelsey presents a carefully reasoned and articulated statement of humanity in Christian theological perspective. He is obviously under the influence of Brunner and Buber, both of whom made an invaluable contribution to our understanding of humanity within the Judeo-Christian tradition. Joseph Washington has observed that Kelsey overlooked the fact that racism is not rational always; sometimes it is irrational. Racism is likewise not always conscious; sometimes it is preconscious.[6] Kelsey addresses directly the racists of the South who are open and frank about their bigotry. Many feel that they have reasonable grounds for their attitudes and practices. They believe that they are good Christians at the same time. But once they are convinced that they are wrong, they may have a radical conversion. Their hatred for blacks turns to a real love for them. Love and hate are both forms of attachment. Once they were against blacks — now they are for them. Kelsey does not help us deal with the indifference of the North.

The racist of the North does not hate the black man; he does know that he exists. Because he ignores the black person's very presence, one is not aware of any race problem or one's complicity in it. There is no need for forgiveness, for one is not conscious of any sin. Even though one is part of the White Power that creates the inner city — the dark ghetto and one's own comforts are explained to a great extent by its existence — the Northern white person does not understand why blacks are angry or the reason for the emergence of Black Power to oppose White Power. Black Theology must awaken such so-called Christians from their peaceful sleep. No white Christian can remain at ease in Zion until blacks are set free.

In presenting this Christian anthropology, Martin Luther King, Jr., looks at Psalm 8:

What is man that thou art mindful of him, and the son of man that thou dost care for him? Yet thou hast made him little less than God, and dost crown him with glory and honor. (Ps. 8:4–5)

King is right in seeing in this statement the biblical basis for the dignity of all human beings. While he goes on to point to the fact that humans are spirit made in the image of God, that they have a rational capacity, that they are free beings and the like, it is on the point of the physical being of humans that King makes special application to racism. He points to the fact that according to the Christian faith, life in the physical body is sacred and significant. Humans do not live by bread alone, but they cannot live without bread either.[7]

King points out the shortcomings of naturalistic and humanistic explanations of human nature that leave out Christian perspectives. He rejects the all too sentimental notions about humanity. Even human shortcomings are explained in terms of errors or lags of nature. The belief that human progress is inevitable and that the human person is gradually evolving into a higher state of perfection is rejected. Freudian terms are used to explain

away human misdeeds. All bad deeds are said to be due to phobias, inner
conflicts — the conflict between the id and the superego. King sees the real
conflict as between humans and God, self and others, resulting from the
estranged relation with God. This is said to be a realistic understanding of
humanity in the light of the Christian faith.[8] It is my view that King's
reflections upon the "misuse" of the Freudian explanation are sound, but
that he might have said something about the constructive contribution of
Freud to Christian understanding as well. The same might be said of Karl
Marx's real contribution to our understanding of human collectivities. Since
a person is an individual and at the same time a person-in-community,
Freud and Marx cannot now be ignored by virtue of their insights into
individuals and society, respectively.

W.E.B. DuBois, in his preface to his fiftieth-year edition of *The Souls of
Black Folk*, makes the point that he had in his original work merely a surface
understanding of the depth of human alienation born of racism, due to the
fact that he had not come to grips with questions concerning human nature
raised by Freud and Marx. Those who admire this classic by DuBois are
pleased that he did not alter *The Souls of Black Folk*. His reason was: "*The
Souls of Black Folk* does not adequately allow for unconscious thought and
the cake of custom in the growth and influence of race prejudice." It is
important, however, that DuBois does realize the weight of the new psychology of Freud and the social utopianism of Marx in the understanding
of human nature.[9]

Black Theology, in its attempt to understand the depths of the blight of
racism upon blacks and whites, will need to be informed not only by the
Christian faith but by the explorations into the unconscious by Freud and
his associates, as well as the analysis of social, economic, and political ills
by Marx and other social philosophers. Whatever insight regarding human
nature may result, will then be taken up into Christian understanding and
transformed by it.

It appears to me that the black theologian has much to learn from existentialism as she or he seeks to develop a helpful understanding of human
nature. When I refer to this self-reflective movement, I do not have par-
ticularly in mind nihilism or pessimism; neither do I cherish its preoccu-
pation with the absurd, with death, or with rebellion. It is not the posture
of existentialists who confront life without God, but the posture of those
who are conscious that humans stand before God, that is most attractive
for the formulation of a Christian anthropology.

Camus, who has found an exalted place in James Cone's Black Theology,
seems to me to be an unfortunate choice. Cone, however, who feels that
black people are to be liberated by "any means necessary," likes the "rebel"
spirit of Camus.[10] It is the Camus of "resistence, rebellion, and death" that
lures Cone on. But Camus, the philosopher of the absurd, the antitheolog-
ical, nonbelieving Camus, who confronts his destiny alone, cannot easily be
"baptized" into the Christian faith. To Camus suicide is physical cowardice
and theology is intellectual suicide. One must admire the prohuman stoi-

cism of Camus—even the defeated person faces death unafraid. But the Christian faith is a religion of hope. Humans are not alone in their struggle for the good, and death is not defeat but an experience of "overcoming the world." There are some insights of value in Camus, Sartre, and others of the prohuman existentialists—those who face life alone without God; but as for me, I find my greatest inspiration in the company of those existentialists such as Pascal, Kierkegaard, and Tillich—these stand before God. This God enables them to overcome aloneness, anxiety, dread, and gives victory over death "the last enemy." Through faith in the God of the resurrection, "threatened being" is no longer under the summons of death.

Existentialists are correct, I believe, in pointing to the finitude and dependency of human beings. They are also correct in lifting up the freedom of persons, their duty to decide, and their responsibility for whatever choices made. According to Tillich, we stand midway between being and nonbeing, and participate in both. Sin is estrangement or separation from God, the Ground of Being. Salvation from this estrangement is reunion; it is overcoming the threat of nonbeing. It is "the courage to be," overcoming the anxiety that is associated with our finitude as persons. Faith is the experience of being seized by the Ultimate. Grace is an acceptance of the fact that we have been accepted even though we are unacceptable.[11] Through this experience one knows the freedom of the Christian person. Through the reunion of the separated—God and humanity, and person and person—health and wholeness come to individuals and communities. Hence, the liberated person is also the reconciled person.

In this representative statement of the possibilities of a Christian understanding of humanity through the existential posture, the black theologian is pointed toward constructive possibilities. The presence of God has meant much to blacks being separated from their homeland, their own kin, and in an alien land among unfriendly people. God has been a "refuge," "a present help in the time of trouble." Standing before God, blacks have been alone, but never lonely. "Walking through the valley of the shadow of death" they "have not feared evil"; for "thou art with me." They have been assured of the intimate companionship of the Shepherd. The Twenty-third Psalm is for blacks an existential message; for God as Shepherd and Host has been a means of triumphing over "threatened being" and has provided meaning for existence. Life requires not merely an "escape" but "meaning" if it is to be fulfilled. Through the Christian understanding of humanity, blacks have discovered not only how to survive; they have determined why they should overcome all the threats to their existence. Thus at the same time we have discovered, through the Christian faith, our dignity as persons, we have also discovered our destiny as a people.

Sin: The Great Separator

Human nature is "a good thing spoiled." Any view that does not account for the "fallenness" of humans is unrealistic. One dealing with others without this assumption is subject to disappointment. Human beings are sinners. This includes black as well as white people. There is a tendency among some black writers to see clearly the sins of whites, but to ignore or overlook the sins of blacks. A Christian realism requires that we be introspective as well as objective in our awareness of the effects of sin upon human nature. This realistic view of humanity enables us to be more understanding and compassionate in our dealings with each other. Pride of goodness on the part of blacks is just as harmful to them as it is to whites who are the prime targets of their criticism. In the words of Paul, we must assert: "all have sinned and fall short of the glory of God" (Rom. 3:23). Sin is universal and therefore must be faced frankly and honestly. Blacks must face their sins and whites must face theirs. Only thus may we understand human nature and assume the task of its remaking with God's help.

What I have said thus far about humans as sinners seems important if we are to have a worthy doctrine of humanity and God at the same time. If we think too highly of humans, we do not need God. If, on the other hand, we think too meanly of humans, the "aliveness of humanity" is overlooked. God is everything; we are nothing. It is, therefore, important to present a God worthy of worship, but a human nature capable of meaningful response to God as a person and not as a puppet. This is important if we are to speak in a helpful manner concerning a subject-subject encounter between God and humans, of real communion between a divine Person and humans on an "I-thou" basis.

Sin is a broken vertical relationship before it is a broken horizontal relationship. There is estrangement between God and humanity, and this explains why each person is set against his or her brother and sister. The Fall comes before the first murder. Sin is the desire to be "as gods." It is self-glory. Sin is misusing the freedom, which is God-given, to say no to the one who makes it possible to say anything. The gift of life is surrounded by the risk of love. God, who is love, creates persons capable of love. These beings are rational and free; they are made in God's own "image and likeness"; they are "a little less than God." A human is able to say no to God. There is a "separableness," an "overagainstness," between God and humanity. If we could not say no, we could not say yes. Without such autonomy of selfhood, humans would not be capable of loving or being loved.

The creation of human life and the risk of love are inherent in God's purpose and activity as a Creator-Spirit. Thus the Fall of humans has first to do with their estrangement from God. God and humans belong together. They are not "strangers"; they are "estranged." Strangers have never met. They come together for the first time. The estranged (as a man and his wife who are separated) overcome separation through reunion. The brokenness between God and humanity is the basis of sin. This includes the sin of racism. Racism is self-glorification of skin color and all the rights and privileges associated with it in a society in which "white is right." Racism is the exaltation of the finite to the status of infinite. Whites desire to be "as gods" to blacks. They are angered if blacks respond, "We call no one father on earth, for our Father is in heaven" (Matt. 23:9).

Sin is also moral evil. Each person is finally a free center of thought and action, even if one must think and act in the context of heredity and environment. Humans experience relative rather than absolute freedom. But human freedom is sufficient to render us inexcusable for our choices. Each person is the "Adam" of his or her own soul. Psychological freedom and moral responsibility are joined. Kant captures this meaning in his celebrated formula: "I ought implies I can." A person, as an autonomous self—free and rational—is faced with a choice between good and evil, even between the lesser of two evils or the greater of two goods. In the light of the knowledge and the ability to make a choice of the best that is possible for us, we deliberately select the less good when a greater good is both known to us and possible for us. Sin is not transmitted through the genes. Original guilt is meaningless on this basis. Guilt is personal only when free choice to sin or not to sin has been exercised by a particular person—not one's ancestors. There is also collective guilt, however.

Racism, in this society, is a situation in which whites are guilty in this collective sense. While whites have the need for repentance for the collective sins and the accompanying guilt of oppression of black people, not all are guilty in a personal sense. When we say that all "whites are racists," do we mean guilty in a personal or collective sense? Racism is so deep-seated, however, on the unconscious level that such a categorical statement concerning guilt may be true to some extent. And then there is the fact of sins of omission as well as those of commission to consider. At this point, blacks as well as whites have reason to enter into serious self-examination. But in a general way, this distinction between personal and collective guilt is to be taken into account as we seek to correct a situation in which blacks are oppressed by whites. Because the individual stands out as "free and responsible," it is possible for one to initiate reforms and set out to right some of the wrongs of the past. Against this background, reparations, restitution, and empowerment considerations begin to make sense to white Christians who may not be aware of being racists themselves but who belong to a race that has inflicted sustained inhuman treatment upon blacks for several centuries. Consciousness of collective guilt does not allow whites to enter into self-pride concerning racism. They should be haunted by the "sins of their fathers and mothers" to such an extent that they would seek to remove the blight of racism upon an entire people in their midst.

Sin as moral evil, as it manifests itself in the brokenness in human relations (between blacks and whites), is personal and social. Blacks as well as whites must reckon with the personal and social directions of sin. Sin is a disability in the individual's life, but it is also a hindrance to reconciliation between persons. In our broken world, sin is the great separator of one ethnic group over against another—of race against race, of class against class.

Sin is centering oneself in self rather than in God. In the area of race, it is difficult for most whites to overcome this deep-seated drive toward the worship of self. A realistic humanism requires blacks to be aware that their own togetherness is shot through with the possibility of exploitation of one another. Under conditions of survival, we often lose any real fellow feeling, any willingness to inconvenience ourselves for the welfare of others. Sin as self-centeredness is a disease that inflicts the black community as well as the white community. Even the black church has not escaped the blight of self-centeredness.

Sin is a type of human bondage. The sinner is not in control of his or her own destiny. Sinners are enslaved by uncontrollable passions, pride, self-centeredness, hate, and the like. The racist, as sinner, is often under the domination of pride of race, inflamed by hatred of other races. He or she is in bondage to his or her prejudices against those in black skin as being inferior to oneself and all those with white skin. When this outlook becomes a way of life, the white person becomes one who lives a sinful life even if he or she is a churchgoer or minister of the gospel. He or she is in bondage to the sin of racism. Regardless of how much he or she testifies to his or her personal salvation, such sinful lives cannot be rewarded with true freedom. One who is to know the true liberty of a child of God must first be reconciled to his or her brother and sister. For blacks it includes those in white skin as well as those in black skin, and for whites it includes those in black skin as well as those in white skin. The brother is everybody.

Until now, black Christians have not been guilty en masse of the sin of racism. A careful look at what this sin has done to large numbers of whites should render it unattractive to those blacks who have not yet chosen such a yoke of slavery. The black theologian has the responsibility of isolating and describing the sin of racism to blacks and whites, but especially to blacks, with the hope that they will not exchange physical oppression for an inner form of oppression—mental, moral, or spiritual.

Being set free from the bondage of the sin of racism is the concern of a theology of freedom. Inner and outer freedom are interdependent. Just as black slaves could not be truly free as Christians while remaining in physical chains, they cannot be free in a physical sense if they embrace the bondage of race hate. This is also the point where liberation and reconciliation meet. Insofar as whites are liberated from the bondage of the sin of racism, they are capable of genuine reconciliation with blacks.

Racism is a stubborn manifestation of sinful self-centeredness. It is personal. Sometimes the individual is aware of pride of race. He or she may be militant and boastful about it. We have already seen what this condition does for the corrosion of personality and the stunting of moral and religious growth. Racism is sinful in an unconscious or preconscious state also. In this form it is insidious and destructive to the self and other selves, but it is most deadly because on the conscious level the white racist is unaware of his or her true condition.

Preconscious racism is a type of "unpardonable" sin, for if one cannot recognize one's sin, if one has no sense of guilt or shame, one does not seek forgiveness through repentance. Whereas the conscious, frank, and boastful racist is in need of a radical conversion experience before he or she is able to accept the black person as equal in nature and grace, the preconscious racist must first be convinced of his or her self-centeredness before being open to the radical change required for reconciliation with his or her brother in black skin. This is never easy, for he or she is often a do-gooder who feels that he or she has already done works beyond a sense of duty to bring the races together. But this type of sin must be overcome if there is to be a breakthrough toward liberation and reconciliation for blacks. And as we have seen, because blacks and whites in this society are so closely associated, whites may never experience liberation and reconciliation unless blacks are included.

Human nature is a good thing spoiled. A human being is a fallen creature. A person is morally neutral. He or she is in a state of becoming one or the other. A person is the "Adam of his or her own soul." A person is free and rational. He or she has been given "the knowledge of good and evil." Sin is vertical—it is a broken relation with God. Sin is horizontal also—it is an estrangement from brother and sister. Sin is moral evil. Sin is personal, but it is also "collective." Guilt likewise is both personal and social. A person is impaired throughout his or her personal and social nature and existence by sin.

Sin is choosing the worst when a better choice is both known and possible. Sin is a form of enslavement from which a person needs to be delivered. Sin is self-centeredness, which includes sensuality and pride—it also includes unrighteousness and self-righteousness. Racism partakes of all known manifestations of sin, both personal and social. American society will never be healthy or whole until this sin has been faced and dealt with. In this task the best of human effort must be supported by the grace and power of God. It will take all that we can do ourselves and all that God by grace and Spirit can bring to pass in and through us to overcome the sin of racism. This must come to pass if blacks are to know true freedom as persons and if there is to be reconciliation between blacks and whites. Sin, the great separator, must be overcome by the love of God that unites persons with God and each other.

The Experience of Forgiveness

Anyone who takes the Christian message of forgiveness seriously, must be open to the possibility that reconciliation between blacks and whites is a possibility. If we realize the difficulty any human being has in performing any pure act, then we may empathize with those whites who honestly seek, at great personal sacrifice, to make amends for wrongs done to their black brothers and sisters. Bitterness and hate are prejudgmental, and when allowed to control one's total outlook, have a tendency to blunt any communication between blacks and whites.

Forgiveness is conditional upon repentance, which involves a change of mind and intention.[12] The purpose is the establishment of a wholesome relationship between persons. In the Old and the New Testaments this point is made. The sacrificial system included offering for sin and guilt. This was a symbolic means by which the taking away of sin involved forgiveness. The giving of the gift was a token of the amends that the repentant sinner expressed. The prophets made the point that no sacrifice availed unless it was supported by sound ethical and humanitarian conduct — turning back to God and a definite change of attitude.

According to Paul forgiveness is closely associated with justification, which includes the elements that make up a right relationship with God. Jesus made the point that there is no limit to forgiveness where there is true repentance (Matt. 18:21–22). Yet he is said to have referred to "an unpardonable sin" — that is, blasphemy against the Holy Spirit. His accusers asserted that he cast out devils by the prince of devils and not by the power of the Holy Spirit. But we overcome the difficulty of the two assertions in apparent tension — on the one hand, forgiveness is limitless; and on the other hand there is unforgivable sin, if we understand Jesus' intention. The "sin to death" (1 John 5:16) refers to that constant state of sin that deadens sensibility beyond the point where one is able to repent. Unrepentable sin is unforgivable just because repentance is a precondition for forgiveness.

According to the Lord's Prayer (Matt. 6:12; Luke 11:4), unless we ourselves forgive, then we have no hope of forgiveness from God. In Matthew 18:21–35 there is an account of a servant who would not forgive his fellow servant a small indebtedness. The master delivered this unforgiving servant to "the tormenters" according to the parable, for he owed his master an enormous debt. Where there is no forgiveness, there is no repentance. If it is true that one who does not repent is not forgiven, it is likewise true that one who cannot forgive others cannot repent, for he or she does not have the sensibility to do so.

The problem confronting whites, even so-called Christians, in reference to blacks is that they cannot repent. Some whites are indifferent to the black person's plight; others assume no responsibility for these adverse conditions. By declaring "I am not a racist," they seek to free themselves of any ties with those of their race who have been and who are currently responsible for the misuse of White Power. Blacks, however, find forgiveness as almost impossible. What whites have done to blacks is so "demonic" that hate and revenge seem to be the only proper attitudes. It is not difficult to understand why Black Muslims refer to whites as "devils" and why religious Black Nationalists often seek to limit love and forgiveness to soul brothers and sisters. But it is sinful not to be able to forgive, just as it is sinful not to be able to repent. Both are unpardonable and are based upon a lack of sensitivity.

Blacks and whites caught up in this bind should look again at Christian salvation as expressed in forgiveness. God has forgiven us our sins, not because we deserve or have earned forgiveness, but because God loves us in spite of our fallenness. A Christian is humbled by the experience of forgiveness. But God's forgiveness is not amoral or sentimental; it is conditioned and moralized—human freedom and responsibility are associated with the manner in which God forgives us. We are to recognize our sinful condition and repent our sins before God "covers" or "removes" them by grace. To have a genuine experience of forgiveness is not merely to be cured of unrighteousness, but of self-righteousness as well. Thus, liberation is a proper precondition for reconciliation in the area of race relations.

It is in the area of group life that blacks and whites most resemble the elder brother of Luke, chapter 15. It is in the realm of ethnic guilt and collective sin that we become most self-righteous in the area of race. An Indian visitor recently pointed to interracial marriage in Indianapolis as an indication of racial harmony. Even if I agreed with him, I would have difficulty finding a healthy reason for interracial marriage in a sick racist society like ours. Given the fact that some interracial couples are not pathological, they still must exist in a society that rejects the union. Interracial marriage does illustrate the possibility of black-white reconciliation on a most intimate basis when it happens on a high level between persons worthy of each other. The individual relationship between two people, even two families, remains an island in an ocean of racial tensions.

We need the kind of collective repentance and forgiveness between blacks and whites that will make it possible for an interracial couple and their offspring to live a happy normal life. Once the white partner was welcomed in the black community and the children of the union were likewise absorbed. The brokenness now prevalent between blacks and whites means that it is doubtful if any interracial couple may be accepted in the black community. They may now expect rejection by both communities. Reaction to interracial marriage on the part of blacks and whites illustrates the sin of self-righteousness in its collective expression. Whites cannot repent and blacks cannot forgive.

Christians do not rely completely on human effort. They are open to the agency of divine grace and power. This is the reason why they dare to hope when otherwise things look hopeless. Never before has reconciliation between blacks and whites in this country been more hopeless. And yet among Christians of both races I see an honest desire for genuine work and life together. There is a point where our Christian faith can lead us beyond the most robust humanism, for we are heirs of a grace that enables as well as sanctifies. To love those who love you is a human act, but to love the oppressor and reject the oppression can be an act made possible by the agency of divine power alone.

A Christian humanism is one in which a person is a co-laborer with God toward his or her own salvation as well as the salvation of others. Even though God's grace enables and sanctifies, we cooperate with God in every stage of personal spiritual growth and in the realization of the will of God in human affairs. This worthy goal requires at the same time persistence and patience. Jesus reminds us of this in his parable of the laborers (Matt. 20:1–16). A householder hired some laborers to work in his vineyard early in the morning. At mid-morning he hired others. At noon and at mid-afternoon he hired still others. Finally he hired some one hour before the close of the day. All were paid a penny. Those who were hired last were paid first also. It seemed so unfair to those toiling all day that they raised a question about just and equal treatment. The point was made. Salvation is a gift; it is not earned. All the laborers received the same thing, for they received more than they were entitled to. God's gift of eternal life is "unspeakable." Beyond all our efforts, God makes the measure full. To realize this should fill our hearts with forgiveness.

Another consideration for a true reckoning with black-white relations from the experience of forgiveness is that there are "tares" among the "wheat" (Matt. 13:24–30). When we are tempted to say all whites are bad and all blacks are good, we should recall this parable. A farmer sowed good seed in good soil, but tares appeared among the wheat. It was observed "an enemy has done this" (Matt. 13:28). When the servants offered to weed out the tares, the master replied that it would not be possible to gather up the tares without uprooting the wheat. Said he: "Let both grow together until the harvest." (Matt. 13:30). Among both blacks and whites there is wheat and there are tares—good and evil. It will be difficult to separate the two, even when we clearly recognize them, before "the time of the harvest." The human condition is a "realistic" and "political" situation. It is one in which there are imperfect strivings; therefore, being forgiven and forgiving others is a constant duty.

Bonhoeffer is right, I believe, when he distinguishes between "cheap grace" and "costly grace," and concludes that according to the best understanding of the Christian faith, grace is never cheap. *Hesed*, "covenant love," in the Old Testament, or *charis*, "divine favor," in the New Testament, is not pity. Pity is "cheap"; it may even involve a certain amount of contempt on the part of the person showing it toward the person receiving it. It needs to be said that much of Christian paternalism expressed by whites toward blacks is in the nature of pity. Grace is a divine attribute. Grace is unmerited favor and is associated theologically with God's redemptive will toward us. It is the free and undeserved act through which God restores estranged creatures to Godself. It is "costly"; for this saving act required the gift of the Son.

Forgiveness and reconciliation come to sinful humanity through the incarnation, which includes the cross and the resurrection. Grace is "costly" and is manifest only when there is an "I-thou" encounter between us and God. Knowing the measure of God's love expressed in God's redemptive act in Christ should humble the Christian and enable one to love and forgive. It should lead the white person to repent of the sin of racism. He or she should realize that the way to God is through reconciliation with the brother and sister. At the same time, it should open the heart of blacks with an honest expression of true forgiveness to those whites who honestly and sincerely repent.

Grace is experienced as a paradox. A combination of human and divine effort is required to lead a Christian life. This means that it takes all we can do for ourselves and all that God can do in and through us to develop our lives toward spiritual fulfillment. Paul captures this "paradox of grace" when he says "Work out your own salvation with fear and trembling; for God is at work in you, both to will and to work for this good pleasure" (Phil. 2:12–13). Thus, as God's grace enables and sanctifies, we are to be "laborers together with God." We are to cooperate toward self-fulfillment and become henceforth agents of reconciliation. The message for blacks and whites in the current polarization of the races seems apparent.

Christ, in his office as priest, mediates to us health and wholeness. Blacks and whites in this racist society have been disabled spiritually, emotionally, mentally, and physically by the sickness and cancerous growth of racism. Its effect has been psychosomatic. It has impaired us as individuals and as groups. It has created anxieties, fears, and hatreds from which we shall have difficulty finding a proper "healing agent." Jesus, who came preaching and practing a program of health, is now addressing this "therapeutic situation." Blacks and whites have developed such a deep pathology that demons must be exorcised. We must be "psychoanalyzed" as well as "socialized." We must open our inner selves to the one who "knows what is in us." The "kingdom is within" and so are the "issues of life," according to Jesus. Blacks talk about "getting ourselves together." Each black person should get himself or herself together in the light of the gospel of Jesus Christ. If we are not healthy, we cannot express health and wholeness abroad.

When we get ourselves together before becoming saviors of the world, we realize that what we have are very few solutions or answers. We do have many questions. But to be able to put the questions in context is a part of the solution. The context of the questions for Christians insofar as racism is concerned is the inner life—the proper relation between oneself and the Lord of Life, even Jesus Christ. From this inner transformation—this "saving" relationship—we may put all else in perspective. It is self-defeating to try to put the world together before we get ourselves together. Our personhood in Christ gives us a base of operation whereby we may affirm the personhood of everyone and participate in making human life more human.

The gospel heals the brokenness within and without. It mends our lives and brings us together.

For black Christians, the Holy Spirit is the one who empowers. Once again, the Holy Spirit is God within the life of the individual Christian and the fellowship of believers in Christ. The Holy Spirit is giver of spiritual life. The Holy Spirit comforts, guides, and strengthens us. We need not make a case for what the Comforter can do for a suffering people, what the guide can do for a lost people, or what the Strengthener can do for a powerless people. The Holy Spirit cultivates and enriches the inner life of the Christian. But the church, as a Spirit-filled community, owes its nature and mission to the presence and work of the Spirit. The church was born through the outpouring of the Spirit. Its nature, message, and mission are dependent upon the Spirit's presence and power. Without the presence of the Spirit, the church is a mere organization or institution. It is another social club or agency. With the Spirit's presence and power, the church is an organism. It is a power for good. It is a hospital for sick souls. It can mend broken lives. It brings succor and comfort to the anxious and the oppressed.

In our racist society, whites are "anxious" and blacks are "oppressed." This "anxiety" accounts for the popularity of psychoanalysis on the part of white preachers and parishioners as well. Often a psychotherapist is added to the ministerial staff. The "couch" is within the church. Affluence is both a "cause" and a "cure" for anxiety among middle-class whites. Without affluence, many anxieties associated with material success would not exist. Without affluence the services of a psychotherapist would not be available. Blacks in "class" congregations suffer from the same "malady," but unless they belong to a "white church" (a church in which blacks are few and powerless), they must seek out a professional couch. Many of these anxieties could be overcome if these people would open their lives up to the presence and power of the Spirit.

Tillich spoke directly to these problems as a theologian. As theologian, he functioned as a priest psychotherapist to the affluent and anxious whites in this racist society. He made us aware of threatened existence, of finitude, and the normal anxieties inclusive in our humanity. He also made us aware of pathological anxieties that required us to go to the couch and be free to "accept the fact that we have been accepted even though we are unacceptable." The "courage to be" requires self-forgiveness as a precondition for divine forgiveness. The Holy Spirit is said to be the one who enables us to overcome the idol worship centered in the self—the cause and seat of our anxieties. The Spirit, as God within, leads us to the experience of "a new being"—a new life through Jesus as the Christ. According to Tillich, worship of the finite self instead of the infinite Ground of Being is the basis of our anxieties.

The black preacher and the black church have always carried on a healing and redeeming ministry. Through sermon, song, and liturgy the black religious experience has been a weekly experience of healing and spiritual inspiration. This appears to be an august tradition rooted in our Afro-American past. Perhaps it has roots in the priest-medicine tradition of Africa. Whatever African influence has survived has been intermingled with our understanding of the Bible and the experience of oppression in these United States. Blacks who copy the religion of the white mainstream, because they have really arrived at a measure of success or make believe that they have done so, have no healing provisions built into their church life. For example, they are less emotional and are more consciously sophisticated in their worship than whites of the same denomination. They are often color-conscious and class-conscious to the extent that blacks with dark skin, little education, and meager means are not welcome. There is often little real fellowship. Most members are trying to show off their affluence through action, speech, or dress. Such an institution is more of a social club than it is a place of worship. Even if the church building is located in the inner city, members have moved to the "Gold Coast." The minister is to be well educated and extremely polished, but he or she dare not extend morning worship for more than an hour. He or she must not introduce any Africanisms into the service—"gospels" and "spirituals" are out. Anthems are in.

The preacher must not get carried away with the message. He or she must present a clear, concise, logical, and cohesive message. Not only must he or she steer clear of emotion in his or her manner of delivery, he or she must not belabor the cause of social justice in the message. It is my impression that this is not the proper climate for the visitation of the Spirit. What cost inauthentic existence! E. Franklin Frazier's apt description of the emptiness and "nothingness" of the "black bourgeoisie" needs not be restated here, for his classic statement goes unchallenged. These blacks have rejected their spiritual home for a promised land they have not been permitted to enter. Dr. King spoke to all blacks, but he also encouraged these blacks as well. By education and culture he was one of them. He had "a dream" of an integrated society. Just before his death, he reported that "from the mountaintop he had seen the promised land." It is only by being oneself that one is open to authentic existence. If we assert the courage to be black, believing that we are adults and not children, that all are one in nature and grace in God's sight, then we are prepared to open our lives and our fellowship to the presence and the power of the Holy Spirit.

I do not advocate emotionalism as an end in itself. I believe that the Spirit visits a Quaker meetinghouse in its stillness as much as a black church in its passionate enthusiasm. Because a person is black and poor does not mean that he or she is heaven bound. Neither does whiteness and great wealth bar a person from the kingdom. Blackness and poverty may lead to bitterness and hatred, or they may lead to sensitiveness to social justice and deep spirituality. After John F. Kennedy, who can say that all persons who are white and wealthy are without social awareness and spiritual perception? It is the quality of life of those who worship that prepares a climate for the presence and power of the Spirit of God, that heals the brokenness within ourselves, within the fellowship, and sends us forth to minister in God's name in a broken world.

All people need an experience of retreat. The Mount of Transfiguration is where we must seek refreshment, perspective, and empowerment. Worship, especially for the oppressed, must be such an exalted experience of spiritual renewal and empowerment. Black worship, composed of gospels, spirituals, sermons, and prayers, must provide refreshment and renewal for travel-weary pilgrims in black skin. "Nobody Knows the Trouble I've Seen" and "Sometimes I Feel Like a Motherless Child" make immediate contact with the black experience. When such pieces are rendered in a white church, they are art; but in a black church, they are worship. When whites and blacks with a white outlook hear these songs, it is for them an aesthetic experience; but when those who are the black poor and those blacks who still remember their own past and who empathize with the present experience of the majority of blacks hear these songs, the Spirit descends — it is a religious experience. Tears drop from their eyes and some say "A-men." The more emotional shout or dance out of their sorrow-joy as the legacy of their bittersweet past unfolds to them as an existential experience. This is a vital part of the experience of forgiveness in the lives of blacks. The experience is so healing and "holing" that it sends the oppressed back into another week of unmerited suffering and enables them to endure it without losing their sanity. Surely a faith that can do this is worth having.

If blacks who are educated have a problem with the absence of the Spirit, the black masses have a problem of presence. This problem of presence is rather a problem of "false identity." We are reminded in the New Testament that we should "test the spirits to see whether they are of God" (1 John 4:1). Most blacks are a religiously gullible people and are available as prey for any "holy" man or woman. This is the reason many young blacks consider religion the biggest con game in the black community. There is no easier road to success. All one needs is a "call" and a way with people. Many charlatans and racketeers have become men and women of the "cloth" in the dark ghetto. Under this religious mantle, they have found their way to fame and fortune. Shielded by religious freedom, they have exploited blacks without running afoul with the law. Any person with the gift of speech and sufficient charisma can sway the black masses. The spiritual leader may even have a "doctor's" degree conferred upon him by a storefront church even if one is functionally illiterate. In the black community as in the early church, it may be said: "Many false prophets have gone out into the world" (1 John 4:1). It is very important, therefore, that the mere expression of vehement emotion not be automatically taken as a manifestation of the Spirit of God.

The early Christians were concerned as blacks must be with the "character" of the Holy Spirit. The presence of the Spirit of God is always a "moralized" presence and power. Jesus, according to the evangelists, was the bearer of the Spirit. The Spirit was present at his baptism. The Spirit gave him power to cast out demons. Jesus tells us that God is a Spirit (John 4:24). The Spirit of God is said to be a spirit of truth (1 John 4:6). The Spirit is an extension of Jesus' mission in the world. The church, as a spirit-filled community, was born in the outpouring of the Spirit at Pentecost. The Spirit was the means by which the apostles carried on their preaching and ministry; for they spoke "as the Spirit gave them utterance" (Acts 2:4). According to Paul, the Spirit gives life (Rom. 8:2). The Spirit is from the God who raised up Jesus (Rom. 8:11). Paul goes on to say:

> The Spirit helps us in our weakness; for we do not know how to pray as we ought, but the Spirit himself intercedes for us with sighs too deep for words. (Rom. 8:26)

Not only are we able to identify the Spirit by his character and saving work, but there are certain evidences of the Spirit's presence and power in the lives of those who have had an experience with the Spirit of God. Thus Paul says: "Now the Lord is the Spirit, and where the Spirit of the Lord is, there is freedom" (2 Cor. 3:17). To be "filled with the Spirit" is to embrace "all that is good and right and true" (Eph. 5:18, 9). To "live by the Spirit" is to "walk by the Spirit" (Gal. 5:25). Those who are "strengthened with might through his Spirit in the inner man" (Eph. 3:16) know "the unity of the spirit in the bond of peace" (Eph. 4:3). They belong to a "fellowship of the Spirit" (Phil. 2:1). The Spirit sanctifies (2 Thess. 2:13). The Spirit also justifies (1 Tim. 3:16).

In these ways we may identify the Spirit of God. The proper identification of the presence and power of the Holy Spirit will enable black Christians to strengthen the inner life and minister in the context of the Spirit's witness to comfort, guide, and strengthen us as we grow in the grace and knowledge of God through Christ Jesus, our Lord. Such an experience of forgiveness should both set us free and bring us together.

6

The Black Messiah

The genius of the Christian religion is that it is at once particular and universal, personal and social. According to the Christian creed, each person is addressed by his or her own name. The question to Adam, "Where are you?" (Gen. 3:9) is put to each and everyone, for each Adam or Eve, each soul. And yet persons in relation to each other are the basis of sociability or fellowship in the community of the faithful. Particularism and universalism both have their place in the context of the Christian faith. The black Messiah encounters the black Christian on the level of personal experience in the black church in its setting in the black community enabling black Christians to overcome their identity crisis—having been alienated, despised, and rejected by the larger community and even in so-called integrated congregations.

I do not take the figure of a black Messiah in a literal historical sense. It is rather a symbol or a myth with profound meaning for black people. It is, therefore, necessary to give some attention to what we mean by a symbol or a myth. I am aware that the definitions of the two terms are different, but it seems to me that in this discussion they will supplement each other.

The word "symbol" is from the Greek word *symbolon*, meaning "token" or "sign." It is also from the Latin *symbolus*, with a similar meaning. It is a token of identity verified by comparing. It stands for something else by reason of relationship, association, or resemblance. It may even be a visible sign of something invisible.[1] It may even be "an object or act that represents a repressed complex through unconscious association."[2] Garth Gillian describes what symbol means in the area of language as follows:

The spoken word is a symbolization in which sound, syntax, and meaning form a living presence which holds within itself a past which escapes its grasp and a future which remains unknown. Or said more simply, that past and that future which remains unknown. Or said more simply, that past and that future are the past and the future of the language community of which the individual is a member.[3]

Symbolism in the area of belief has been aptly described by Edwyn Bevan as follows:

> A symbol ... means something presented to the senses or the imagination ... which stands for something else. Symbolism in that way runs through the whole of life. Every moment we are seeing objects or hearing sounds or smelling smells which bring to our minds a vast complex of things other than themselves—words, for instance, as spoken or written signs. And if symbolism thus runs through life as a whole, it is a factor of the first importance in religion.[4]

From this understanding of a symbol and the meaning that symbolism has in all of life, it is not difficult to understand the use to which a symbol like the black Messiah may be put. But before pursuing this logic, we will take a similar look at myth.

The word "myth" comes from the Greek *mythos*. It may be a traditional story of historical events that serves to unfold part of the worldview of a people or explain a practice, belief, or natural phenomenon. It may describe a person or thing having only an imaginary or unverifiable existence.[5]

Charles Long, in his book *Alpha: Myths of Creation*, refers to myth as a true story about reality. According to him, it is impossible to understand a people unless we understand what is real to them in relation to myth, their reality in the precise sense of their human presence, their "qualitative meaning in time and space."[6]

Myth is not primarily logical, but it is not illogical or prelogical either. It is a type of thinking that is at once logical and illogical, logical and magical, rational and irrational. It is concerned with the human "initial confrontation with the power in life."[7] It has to do with an individual's or a people's reaction to life as a source of power and being. "The word and content of myth are revelations of power."[8]

According to Long, the mythical and rational coexist. Alongside the rational, the mythical remains a mode through which we have access to the real. Modern cultural life identifies truth and literalness. This results partly from the scientific-technological character of our culture. Long reminds us that we do not live entirely in a world of literal meanings.[9] When my three-year-old daughter presented me with something to eat that I could not, she shook me out of my literal world into her imaginary or mystical world by saying, "Daddy, pretend that you are eating." Once I had pretended that I had eaten what she offered me, she was satisfied and went back to her play. The move out of the adult world of literal meanings into a small child's world of mythical meanings is part of what myth is all about.

There are human experiences that are "profound"—not merely "immature" or "childish," both personal and cultural—which may only be expressed in symbolic forms. These meanings are in many cases the most profound meanings in our personal and cultural lives. Long sums up his discussion thus: "They are profound because they symbolize the specificity of our human situation—they make clear to us and point up the resources and tensions which are present in our situation."[10]

Long goes on to make contact with our interpretive interest in myth in this way:

> In philosophy and theology, the use of analogy may be an attempt to deal discursively with the more profound symbolic forms of human expression. The adequacy of analogy as theological and philosophical tool lies at the heart of the "de-mythologizing" problem in theology today.[11]

Susanne K. Langer brings preliminary discussion on myth to a close as she says:

> Myth . . . is a recognition of natural conflicts, of human desire frustrated by . . . hostile oppression, or contrary desires; it is a story of birth, passion, and defeat by death which is man's common fate. Its ultimate end is not wishful distortion of the world, but serious envisagement of its fundamental truths; moral orientation . . . It presents . . . a world-picture, an insight into life generally . . . Because the mythological hero is not the subject of an egocentric day-dream, but a subject greater than any individual, he is at least a descendant of the gods, something more than a man. His sphere of activity is the real world, because what he symbolizes belongs to the real world.[12]

Christology, the person and work of Christ, is the fortress of the Christian faith. Anyone with the Christian faith-claim has to have good reasons for a radical restatement of a doctrine so central to the Christian creed. My use of symbol and myth in the understanding of the black Messiah does not mean that I am prepared to give up a historical-literal understanding of the incarnate Lord. My study of Hinduism with its several *avatars*, or "embodiments" of Vishnu and Shiva has made me very much aware of the precious nature of incarnation, the "word made flesh" in Jesus as the Christ. Hindus speak of incarnations. Christians believe in one incarnation—that "God was in Christ reconciling the world to himself" (2 Cor. 5:19). Christ is the center of our faith. Light, life, and truth from God are revealed supremely and uniquely in and through the incarnate Lord.

Our concern is psychocultural. We are attempting to particularize God's redemptive act in a special human situation. Jesus as the Christ is the "desire of all nations," but he is also the savior of each person and every people. Christ needs to speak to black people in their situation and in terms of a "black presence" in their midst. The epiphany of Christ is among black people and, as of old, Jesus promises to be with us always.

When Emil Brunner visited Japan, the Japanese theologians said to him,

"Leave us alone with Christ." Recently I spoke to Dr. Tetsutaro Ariga, of Nishinomiya, Japan, about mutual friends in Japan. I wanted to know from him about the indigenization of theology among Japanese theologians. We were in Geneva at a summit conference on world religions. As a distinguished Christian scholar, Dr. Ariga shares with me the interest in the encounter between Christianity and non-Christian religions. Thus I knew that he had given considerable thought as to how the Christian faith needs to express itself in a culture in which Christians are in a minority and in which non-Christian religions such as Shintoism, Buddhism, and Confucianism are more predominant. Dr. Ariga surprised me by pointing out that too many Japanese theologians were so busy trying to keep up with what Western theologians are saying that they are not able to get on with this important task of indigenizing the Christian faith.

I was pleasantly surprised upon my return to find in my mail a copy of the *Northeast Asia Journal of Theology* entitled "Toward a Theology of Indigenization." This means that some theologians in Taiwan, Korea, and Japan are working hard at the task of relating theological knowledge to the cultural situation of Christians in East Asia. The article by Prof. Nam Dong Suh on "The Contemporaneous Christ" is most attractive. Dr. Suh, of Korea, was trained in Japan and Canada. In his article theological insights of East and West meet, but the burden of his message is to acquaint Korean Christians with the meaning of Christ for them. Christian scholars in many lands are busy with the task of indigenizing the Christian faith. This is going on in India, in Africa, and in Latin America. The reason for this is that the Westernized Christ presented by Western missionaries and interpreted by Western theologians, mostly white and puffed up with pride of race and culture, did not speak and act redemptively in the Third World. A part of the personhood of Christians in the Third World is the request to be "left alone with the Christ."

Black Theology has every right to make the same request. The Christ of the slave master is not an adequate Christ for freed blacks who affirm their dignity and freedom as children of God. Vincent Harding is correct: the "Americanized Christ," who has been acculturated into a white middle-class image, is not the black person's Christ. The Americanized Christ, as created by the majority group in this country, is found in all artistic presentations of Christ to be a WASP.[13] In other words, there is a preconscious assumption that if Christ is to be worthy of devotion, he must be a member of the white race. Those who criticize Cleage and other black scholars who seek to correct this situation should first recognize what gave rise to the need for a black Messiah. It is always easier, however, to criticize others than it is to enter into self-criticism. I do not need to agree with Cleage's version of the black Messiah to see the need for a black understanding of christology. Since the black experience has been disregarded in other versions of christology, there is a need to make Christ and his message speak directly to the black person.

Think what Christ must look like to an Indian, a Japanese, or an African who has not been introduced to the savior by a white Westerner or a Westernized native. The picture of Christ as being one of them does not preclude the possibility that he may relate to others also. Only in this sense may he be Christ for all people. This is the area where psychology and theology meet. Dr. Kurt F. Leidecker, in a recent lecture on Buddhist symbols, pointed out that the features of the Buddha in sculpture and painting mimic the ethnic origin of the artist, so that a Burmese artist will give the Buddha Burmese features, a Chinese artist Chinese ones. The only exception, Dr. Leidecker found, was in the Sukhothai style of art in Thailand, where artists endeavored to find out what the people in the area in which the Buddha was born and lived looked like.[14] The point is made. Most people will depict the image of the ultimate in the visible form native to their own culture and ethnic group. It follows that the white Americanized Christ is alien to black people and this is the reason for the search for a black Christ.

The visualization of Christ as black may enable the black person to have a real encounter with self and God through Christ. The black person has in the black Messiah a savior. He or she discovers his or her own dignity and pride in a self-awareness that is rooted in black consciousness. Christ conceived in a black image is one of us and in a real sense becomes our Lord and our God. Like Thomas, the doubter, the black person may now cry out in pride and joy to the black Messiah, "My Lord and my God!" His or her experience does not preclude the possibility that others may have the same vital experience in a varied ethnic and cultural setting. The black Messiah is also the universal word made flesh. I do not support the view that Christ is actually black in a literal-historical sense. Therefore, I wish to disassociate myself from Cleage's attempt to establish a literal black Messiah on historical grounds.

The appearance of a black Madonna in Europe is art. But the appearance of the same symbol, to blacks in Africa or America in search of a savior, is religion. The interpretation of the former is aesthetics, while the understanding of the latter is theology. It follows that I do not suggest that white people repent for worshiping a Christ in their own image to worship one in my likeness. The worship of a white Christ has dehumanized black people. The worship of a black Christ, for the same reason, would dehumanize white people. We would be confronted with a false identity in both instances and thus to exchange one false identity for another would not be an improvement.

To overcome the charge of fostering separatism as an end in itself, I will suggest that this could be done for a different reason—for reconciliation between equals. The former (adoration of a black Messiah by blacks) is for liberation—to enable an oppressed people to go free. If white Christians can overcome color consciousness and the inferiority-superiority syndrome associated with it to the extent that they are able to worship a black Christ, then perhaps reconciliation is nearer than we first believed. There is too much pathology in society, however, for the theologian to recommend further sickness. If the reason for suggesting that white people worship a black Christ is because of what a white Christ has or has not meant to the black person, then our motive would appear to be revenge or punishment. This is a negative approach to a black Messiah. This is not a proper motive for a worthy christological statement. Only unhealthy whites, characterized by a masochistic enjoyment of being abused and dominated as a release from the torment of a guilt-ridden spirit, will be impressed by this interpretation. There would, on our part, be an element of sadism if the intention were merely to "repay whites" or inflict pain. Reconciliation between equals based upon equal mutual respect is the only premise upon which blacks and whites may transcend the "skin color" of Christ and thereby worship the universal Christ. The experience of reconciliation is not pathological but "holing" and healing to the reconciled.

A universal Christ will be as "existential" to red, yellow, and black people as he is to white people. One of the reasons why I would resist the affirmation of a black Christ to the exclusion of a white Christ is that this would likewise exclude a yellow Christ and other skin colors in which the existential Christ may confront humans in a cultural-historical setting. Many oppressed people in the Third World are not white, but they need the Christ of the oppressed just as much as we do. In our present excitement over Pan-Africanism, we should not forget large numbers of colored oppressed people are not in Africa or North America, but in Asia, Latin America, and the islands around the globe. If we give our christology the right shape, we may be helpful in making Christ the "desire of all nations." In one sense Christ must be said to be universal and therefore colorless. Only in a symbolic or mythical sense, then, must we understand the black Messiah in the context of the black religious experience.

A symbol participates in that which it symbolizes while it also points beyond itself as mere symbol. Against this assertion, we may make certain affirmations. The black Christ participates in the black experience. In some sense Christ makes contact with what the black Christian is aware of in his or her unique history and personal experience. He or she encounters Christ in that experience and is confronted by the claims of Christ also in his or her black experience. But at the same time, the confrontation of the black Christian with the black Messiah, who is also the universal Christ, points him or her beyond the mere symbolism that is rooted in experience. In other words, the universal Christ is particularized for the black Christian in the black experience of the black Messiah, but the black Messiah is at the same time universalized in the Christ of the gospel who meets all persons in their situation. The black Messiah liberates the black person. The universal Christ reconciles the black person with the rest of humankind.

It was Sören Kierkegaard who introduced in an explicit manner the idea of the "contemporaneity" of Christ into modern theology. But as the father of existentialism, he was primarily interested in the category of the "individual" and not of collective humanity. He was opposing mass movement in church and state, which repressed the "crown rights of individuals." Black Theology is interested in individual rights, but it has real concern for the rights of all blacks. We may, therefore, only assume the existential posture of Kierkegaard, but recognize the difference between his situation and ours.

The idea of Christ as a contemporary erases the temporal distance between Christ and us. Christ's deeds and words come home to us in the "living present." Howard Thurman, the distinguished black mystic and preacher, is aware of the affinity between Jesus' life, ministry, and death and the "facts of life" for the black people. In his *Jesus and the Disinherited*, Thurman repeatedly illustrates the saving relationship between Jesus and "the disinherited" — the blacks, the poor, those who represent the "oppressed." Thurman, like Albert Cleage, feels such a closeness to Jesus that Paul, for him, does not present a religion *of* Jesus, but a religion *about* Jesus. Thurman did most of his work before the emergence of the latest black revolution, and hence the language of Black Theology is foreign to his interpretation of religious experience. His interpretation of why Jesus is admired by the oppressed anticipates any worthy understanding of the black Messiah.

When white law-and-order-without-justice politicians speak of the forgotten American or the silent majority, they have in mind white people. The black person has always been the forgotten one in this country. In the language of James Baldwin, "nobody knows my name." He or she is minus a name and has no personal identity or significance. He or she can be called anything at any time. A seventy-year-old man is a "boy." My name is "Jack," "fellow" — whatever the white person decides to call me. I know, for "my face is black." It is the black person who knows what it really means to be nameless, anonymous, in this country. In the spring of 1970, four white students were shot in a demonstration at Kent State University. This incident, along with the expansion of the war into Cambodia, was enough to paralyze most colleges and universities in the land. Black people remembered the death of black students at South Carolina State College at Orangeburg a few years back with little concern expressed by whites. A few days after the Kent killings, six black men were shot in the back by National Guardsmen in Augusta, Georgia, with little notice. When will Americans learn that all life is sacred and equally precious?

The black Christian as he or she experiences suffering, rejection, and loneliness in a white racist society needs a savior who knows his or her name — a redeemer who individualizes love. The black Messiah comes to his or her own; he calls each black person by name. Through faith Christ becomes a contemporary of the black person. The black Messiah is right here, right now, and he is one who understands our need because he is one of us. But the Christ who is our contemporary, who confronts us as the black Messiah, does not confirm us in our sin and immorality; he asks us to change our lives. In and through the black Messiah, the good news of salvation is presented to us in our own dialect in terms and ideas that are familiar to us as black persons. The black Messiah meets us against the background of our history and our culture. He speaks to us in the language of "soul." "My Lord and my God" is the response of the black person who has been in search of a redeemer. Christ is Lord, just as much to the present Christian as he was to the disciples, if through faith he becomes our contemporary. The black Christ, the Christ of the black person's faith, is with the black person in his or her experience of oppression at the hands of the white person.

My own understanding of christology is that of my teachers with some reinterpretation based upon my experience as a black person. It is informed by the experiences of the suffering race to which I belong. The shape of christology for me is inspired by British neoliberal theologians such as John Baillie and Herbert Farmer, both of whom were my teachers, the former at Edinburgh University and the latter at Cambridge University. But it is the christology of Donald Baillie's *God Was in Christ* that has made a permanent impression upon my statement of christology. Emil Brunner's *The Mediator* has had a remarkable influence upon my mind also. Rudolf Bultmann has impressed me to some extent. This has not been so much a direct influence as it has been an indirect influence of John Macquarrie's critical evaluation of Bultmann's program. Macquarrie combines, as I understand him, a good understanding of Heidegger and Bultmann with sound Reformation theology and Scottish "common sense." Macquarrie's suggestion that the "existential Christ" must also be historical, that subjective faith and objective verification must be combined in a valid christology, seems rather sound. Add to this Donald Baillie's conclusion that the Jesus of history is the Christ of faith and one sees a tenable pattern for a sound statement on the person and work of Christ. This is only a hint at the direction a purely christological statement would take for the present writer. Since we are concerned here primarily with the form which a valid understanding of Christ will take for blacks, I need not pursue this matter further. The frame of reference is the black Messiah; the content will be "the Jesus of history as the Christ of faith."

The essence or content of christology has to do with the heart of the proclamation of good news centered in the cross and resurrection. Biblical revelation that moves from promise to fulfillment has unusual vitality in the affirmation of faith as applied to the black experience. Egyptian bondage, the land of promise, exile, restoration, the prophetic word, the messianic hope, the coming of Christ, the beloved community, the new age — all are pivotal concepts centered in the Christian message of redemption. All make a profound impact upon the black religious experience. This may explain why the humblest black Christian seems to take the Christian faith more seriously than those who introduced it. It is a miracle of history and of grace that a people brought to the New World in chains, in a ship called Jesus, piloted by a captain who penned the hymn "How Sweet the Name of Jesus Sounds," can still use that hymn with great fervor and meaning.

It was as if they were given a deep insight into the meaning and message of the incarnation, not in spite of what happened to them but because of their unmerited suffering. Such penetrating understanding of the real meaning of the doctrine of Christ may revive what some have made a lifeless and sterile belief. No one can fully understand the revelation of God if he or she does not know the meaning of the cross, not merely as unmerited suffering but also as a healing balm. Others may have to seek a cross, but as for the black person, the cross finds, follows, and haunts blacks. The cross is a primary and not a tertiary experience for blacks. Some Christians may have only a secondhand experience of this cross. They may take it up and lay it down at will. Through compassion or charity they may share the cross of the oppressed, but the oppressed bear an involuntary cross. The black person shoulders a cross at birth and never emerges from its burden. It is an existential cross. The cross is understood by blacks in terms of personal pronouns:

> But he was wounded for our transgressions,
> he was bruised for our iniquities;
> upon him was the chastisement that made us whole,
> and with his stripes we are healed. (Isa. 53:5)

In an understanding of the cross from the vantage point of black consciousness, the black Christian experiencing the revelation of God through the black Messiah bears an existential cross. This is the reason why the hymn "Must Jesus Bear the Cross Alone?" is sung by blacks with so much emotion and meaning. When the hymn says, "no, there is a cross for everyone, and there is a cross for me," it goes right to the heart of the black religious experience.

The black Christian knows that grace is never cheap. When I was a boy, I used to hear older blacks sing in the black church: "I wonder what makes this race so hard to run?" Those Christians knew the meaning of suffering. They knew that grace is never cheap. Blacks know what it means to suffer with Christ and share his agony. Like Paul many blacks "bear on their bodies the marks of Jesus" (Gal. 6:17). The rejection and shame of the crucifixion, which Bonhoeffer recounts so profoundly in his *The Cost of Discipleship*, is integral to the black experience. When I was a boy I used to hear older people give the gruesome details of lynchings that took place in our Southern town in the presence of horrified blacks. They knew the meaning of cross-bearing. As an adult, I too have known in my own experience what it means to endure harsh treatment and unmerited suffering in black skin in a racist society. In the midst of these experiences, the cross has been to me a healing cross.

Carrying the cross may be for the black Christian a bittersweet experience. It is bitter because it is burdensome; it is heavy. The cross involves suffering, shame—even death. But the cross is also revelatory of the love of God—of "love divine, all loves excelling." It is through the window of the cross that we see the face of God. And the God who is revealed through the cross is just, righteous, and loving—mighty to save. The black person bears an involuntary cross. It follows that he or she must deal with the cross. What makes the difference is his or her response to the cross and its meaning for the life one derives from it. The cross will make or break one. It will either provoke one to great bitterness or mellow one's spirit to great depths of compassion. Everything depends upon whether the *agape* of the cross triumphs over its suffering and shame.

This is the reason why the cross and the resurrection are often referred to as one event in God's redeeming mission in the world. The resurrection is the sequel to the cross. Without Easter morning, Good Friday would be Bad Friday, for evil would have the last word.

It is the existential resurrection that breaks through with meaning. The black person's problem with christology has little to do with proving or disproving the historical resurrection. For the most part, black Christians take the historicity of the resurrection with all seriousness. So much depends upon the resurrection and its power. The resurrection is central to the New Testament faith. It was the central theme of apostolic teaching and preaching. The witness of the primitive Christian church was founded upon the assurance that "God has made him both Lord and Christ, this Jesus whom you crucified" (Acts 2:36).

For black Christians the resurrection has much to say about God's direction of human affairs. It reveals God's providence as well as God's salvific work among humans. A righteous, just, merciful, loving, powerful God still runs history. At the cross, evil at its worst confronted holiness at its best, and love won the victory over hate. Because of resurrection power, life has triumphed over death. In the black person's understanding of the resurrection, the sacred and the secular merge. When one witnesses: "I know he [Christ] lives, for he lives in my soul," it means that one's own spiritual condition has changed—that one has died to sin and been raised (redeemed) to a new style of living. Something like the Pauline "mystical union" with Christ is implied. But a new age has come into being, God's new age. The climax of a struggle for justice and righteousness in history has occurred and the victory belongs to God. The resurrection has a personal, existential, saving message for the black Christian as an individual, but it also has a historical, collective, political, and providential message for black people as a church, as a race. The resurrection is the basis of a black hope secure in the God of the resurrection, who is a God of love and power, who promises to be with us always and to make all things new.

The three offices of Christ as prophet, priest, and king have real meaning for a theology of liberation and reconciliation. As prophet, the black Messiah stands as the fulfillment of all Biblical prophecy. The prophet as spokesman for God is represented most completely in Jesus as the Christ. Jesus spoke words of harsh judgment against the political and the religious establishment. He condemned evil wherever it was found, whether among the Romans or among the Jews, his own people. Black theologians and preachers must do likewise if they are to stand in the tradition of the Biblical prophets. We must condemn wrongdoing whether among our own people or among those who oppress us. The prophetic word will have a different message for blacks over against whites, but if we follow the example of Jesus as prophet, we must speak within as well as without.

The black Messiah heals wounds. The Jesus of the Gospels restored sight to the blind. He made the lame to walk. As a result of his healing touch, lepers were cleansed, the dumb spoke, and the lonely found true friendship. Christ is priest to the oppressed, the imprisoned, the outcast. In his presence, those alone were no longer lonely; those bound were set free; those who mourned were comforted. In his healing ministry he consoled those who were troubled, distressed, and disturbed. Christ comes to the black person as the black Messiah and ministers among us as priest. He makes black people aware of a benevolent and provident God who watches over all and is no respecter of persons. The black Messiah identifies with us in his compassion. He speaks to black persons in slum dwellings, in alleys, and in the byways of dark ghettos. He speaks to the black sharecropper in his poverty, misery, and need. As the universal Christ, he speaks to the oppressed everywhere in their own language and in their situation.

Christ is king. A king must have a kingdom. His kingdom is not of this world. It is within. He reigns over a realm of moral and spiritual ends. His kingdom exists wherever the will of God is done and to the extent that the will of God has come to a point of realization. The black Messiah comes into the black experience as one who reigns. As Lord he has power over all history and all creation. He unseats the mighty from their thrones and exalts the helpless and the hopeless. The destiny of the weak and powerless is safe in his sovereign trust. He empowers the powerless; he invests black persons with dignity. As the black Messiah, he addresses them as sons and daughters, and as heirs with himself for the kingdom of God—the kingdom that God has prepared for all who love him. The kingship of Christ as the black Messiah has great merit for lifting up the aspirations of the oppressed. Black people are still an oppressed and long-suffering people. The black Messiah brings good news to the black person, "glad tidings of redemption and release." The black Christian is assured: "So through God you are no longer a slave but a son, and if a son then an heir" (Gal. 4:7).

The kingship of the black Messiah is present as well as future. This black hope of liberation in the present and reconciliation in the future is summed up in the ministry of Christ as king:

Then comes the end, when he delivers the kingdom to God the Father after destroying every rule and every authority and power. For he must reign until he has put all his enemies under his feet. (1 Cor. 15:24–25)

The theme of Christ the liberator is a popular one at present among black theologians and preachers. It has been treated so well by others that it need not be given extensive treatment here.[15] James Cone says: "Jesus' work is essentially one of liberation. Becoming a slave himself, he opens realities of human existence formerly closed to man."[16]

Bishop Joseph A. Johnson, Jr., has referred to Paul's experience of the new life as one of liberation. Says Johnson: "The liberating power of Jesus had emancipated him and set him free."[17] Johnson's discussion is a work of obvious scholarship in the New Testament. As a former New Testament professor, as church administrator, and as chairman of the theological commission of the National Committee of Black Churchmen, Johnson has made a real contribution to a christological statement of the black religious experience that will be illuminating and meaningful to black Christians. But at the same time, because he is in touch with the best scholarship in New Testament studies, all scholars will gain depth of understanding by reading him. Johnson says:

> Jesus, the Liberator, had given Paul not only freedom but also a new self-understanding. . . . Paul discovered that he who belongs to Jesus, the Liberator, and thus to God has become master of everything. He declares to the Christians at Corinth that this grace-freedom event which they had experienced in Jesus, the Liberator, placed the world at their disposal . . . "all things are yours; and you are Christ's; and Christ is God's." (1 Cor. 3:22–23)[18]

Johnson's appreciation of Paul's contribution to an understanding of the Christian faith is refreshing. As a New Testament scholar, he has been able to overcome the distortions to which white preachers and scholars have put Paul's message in the history of black oppression. Paul may have been misguided, but he was, nevertheless, a man of great moral courage. He did not speak out against slavery; he was an intellectual, an aristocrat, a Roman citizen, and so on. But he was a man of great conviction as well. He suffered and was willing to die for what he believed. He was a moral, intellectual, and spiritual genius. His letter to the Galatians may rightly be called the Magna Carta of the Christian. No adequate statement of liberation or of Christ as liberator can be derived from the New Testament that does not consider carefully Paul's message of Christian freedom. Black theologians who must deal with liberation as a cardinal concern will do well to follow Bishop Johnson's worthy example.

Johnson is not naive concerning the misuse of the Bible in the area of race. He is aware that white theology has not presented an adequate message for blacks. According to Johnson, it has not been able to reshape the life of the white church so as to cleanse it of racism and to liberate it from the iron claws of the white racist establishment of this nation."[19]

There is a need to discover a black Messiah, a black Christ, according to Bishop Johnson, because the white Christ of the white church is the enemy of the black person. This Christ is the oppressor of blacks. Thus the black preacher and the black scholar are duty bound "to discover Christ in his or her image of blackness."[20] To this end black scholars must not abandon the Christian faith or the biblical record; they must reread the Bible and they must "detheologize" the faith so that the Christian message will speak to their situation with "a disturbing clarity."[21] He tells us what detheologizing demands. We must rediscover the humanity of Jesus.[22] He refers to the "Jesus [who] was born in a barn, wrapped in a blanket used for sick cattle, and placed in a stall. He died on a city dump outside Jerusalem."[23]

Jesus is the liberator. The theological commission of the National Committee of Black Churchmen, in its Atlanta document of June 1969, to which Bishop Johnson and the present writer made a contribution, declared Christ to be "the Liberator" and Black Theology to be "the theology of black liberation." But the statement says little about reconciliation. It does say, however, that insofar as blacks are liberated, whites will "affirm" their own humanity. Black Theology has an awesome task. While we speak externally to liberation from white oppression, we must speak internally to the need for forgiveness from sin and exploitation within our own group life. Black Theology must speak of liberation within from blacks and liberation from without from whites. But at the same time, it must speak of reconciliation that brings blacks together and of reconciliation that brings blacks and whites together, both in a multiracial fellowship of the body of Christ and within the world where a multiracial society must be built.

This means that Christ the Liberator is also Christ the Reconciler. Christ is the one "who brings us together." We remember the promises of President Nixon as he sought the highest office in the nation. His promise was "to bring us together." Within a few months after his election, we discovered that we had never been so far apart. Perhaps this was only a "political promise," which no one should have taken seriously in the first place. Perhaps it was a promise based upon lack of foresight, lack of resources, and lack of knowledge. All human promises are fallible and finite. But in and through Christ, God promises "to bring us together." This is a promise that God can and will keep. Christ liberates, but he also reconciles us to God and to each other.

His cross is a reconciling cross. Black Christians have borne their cross through the years. They know the meaning of unmerited suffering. They now can carry on a ministry of reconciliation across the generations and between races and nations—and become agents of healing in a broken world.

Up to the day of the cross, the best understanding we had of God was the father of a wayward son. He waited daily, prayerfully, for his son's homecoming. Underneath the repentance of the son was the conviction that he could count on his father. Dignity, freedom, and love represent God's attitude toward us. The cross goes deeper. It demonstrates how humans may be brought back to the heart of God. We kneel at the cross; we are changed by its power. The cross is the supreme revelation of God's love for us. The cross does not merely indicate the true character of God; it also shows the resistance of sin and evil to the love of God. Because of sin, human nature had been twisted and perverted. Even physical nature, all creation, had been thrown out of joint, so Paul could say, "the whole creation has been groaning" (Rom. 8:22). Thus E.D. Burton could say: "The suffering of Christ on the cross is the momentary laying bare of the agelong hurt sin inflicts on the heart of God."[24]

The cross reflects God's estimate of humanity. God wants us more than we want God. Humans are worth dying for; we are worth the life of the Son of God. The cross is the best revelation of God; it plumbs the depths of sin and evil, and it manifests the infinite value God places upon human life. God, sin, and humanity must meet in the cross. At the very place where God's love is violated, one comes to grips with sin and evil. But at the same place, God draws persons into harmony with the love and the purposes that flow from it. Christ is the reconciler and the ministry of the cross is reconciliation.

This leads us to say that when we discover Christ as the black Messiah, as the one who enters into our black experience, the meaning of the cross and our suffering is reconciliation. The reconciliation of person to person, through the reconciliation of humanity to God, releases the healing power of the cross of Christ into this anxious, broken, and bitter world. Only redeemed persons can serve as agents of reconciliation. All who would serve as reconcilers must themselves be persons of integrity. On the cross Christ gives himself to humankind. Black men and women, reconciled to God through the cross of Christ, but who through their suffering, their own cross-bearing, share the depth of his suffering, are purified, mellowed, and heightened in sensitivity and compassion. Thus healed and released in their own life, they may now become healers of others. The God, who through Christ reconciles the world to Godself, sends us forth to be agents of reconciliation. To such a witness in a broken world, blacks may not only be "called," but indeed "chosen."

While other scholars continue upon the quest for the "historical Jesus" and as they continue the "new quest," the black theologian's quest is for the black Messiah, the Liberator of black people, the Reconciler of humans to God and each other. Our search has led us to our situation. Others will find the messiah in theirs. In the end we long for the universal Christ, who will not only set us free, but bring us together. Albert Schweitzer, who found the Christ, not in intellectual research for his *Quest of the Historical*

Jesus but in his service as medical missionary in Africa, sums up the nature of our quest of the Jesus of history who is also the Christ of faith:

> He comes to us as One unknown, without a name, as of old, by the lake-side. He came to those men who knew Him not. He speaks to us the same word: "Follow thou me!" and sets us to the tasks which He has to fulfil for our time. He commands. And to those who obey Him, whether they be wise or simple, He will reveal Himself in the toils, the conflicts, the sufferings which they shall pass through in His fellowship, and, as an ineffable mystery, they shall learn in their experience Who He is.[25]

Listen to Bishop Johnson again:

> The people of all races, because of his service, are able to identify with him and to see in his humanity, a reflection of their own images. Today the black man looks at Jesus — observes his ministry of love and liberation and considers him the black Messiah who fights oppression and sets the captive free.[26]

This is precisely the black Messiah.

7

Hope—Now and Then

The so-called theology of hope has a good psychological ring for a hope-less people. It does not, however, ring true to the black experience. Like many other "transport" theological movements, it belongs to another "sit-uation." Insofar as it speaks directly to the Marxist-Christian dialogue, it will find "domestication" in white America difficult also. The "political" and "revolutionary" aspects of the theology of hope are addressed primarily to the Third World as it confronts a postcolonial period of development. This latter aspect of the theology of hope may be examined with profit by the interpreter of the Christian faith to black people who belong essentially to the oppressed of humankind.

Eschatology for blacks must be both *realized* and *unrealized*. Whereas the evangelical-pietistic version of eschatology is preoccupied with the future, Black Theology must begin, I believe, with the present. In other words, for black Christians realized eschatology, the manifestation of the will of God in the present—abstractly as social justice and concretely as goods and services to "humanize" life—must be a first consideration for a doctrine pointing to the eventual consummation of God's purposes in creation and history. Those messianic and apocalyptic versions of eschatology centering on heaven and hell, future punishments and rewards, the resurrection of the flesh, will become less and less attractive to black people struggling to survive, even under the threat of genocide, here and now. Promise of future awards or punishments make little impression. Heaven as a reward at some unforseeable future time brings little hope to the hungry and mistreated black person. Hell-future makes little impression upon blacks living in hell-present of shacks, rats, roaches, hunger, unemployment, and inhuman treat-ment. The resurrection of the flesh is bad news for blacks who suffer so much undeserved pain in the present body. The same is true of any human who endures great suffering in the flesh. To carry the pain and agony of a feeble body beyond the grave would be for these the promise of an "eternal cross." Those who have found life in this world—specifically in the flesh fulfilled—may long for the "resurrection of the flesh."

While eschatology, from the Greek *eschatos*, "last" or "farthest," refers to belief in the end of the world or last things (that is, second coming of Christ, resurrection, judgment, the new age), it must also refer to "present things" for blacks. Instead of moving from the future to the present, we move from the present to the future—at least to begin. Only after we are aware of what God is doing in this world to make life more human for blacks, may we speak of God's future breaking into our present and look forward to the new age.

The most helpful treatment of the question of eschatology for blacks, known to me, is the book by Rubem A. Alves, *A Theology of Human Hope*.[1] Alves is a theologian of the Third World. He has a social consciousness that is refreshing. As a "colored" theologian from a country preoccupied with development, exploited by white nations, beset by violent social revolutions, he can dig oppression and is sympatic to the Afro-American experience.

Alves needs to realize that there is little relation between New Left students who want a coed dorm and black students who want a black cultural center. These white students are reacting to "a generation gap." They want to break with social and moral conventions. This is what liberation means to students who have the means to spend their Christmas vacation in the Virgin Islands and on beaches in Florida, and their summers in Europe or Asia. But liberation to black students means an affirmation that they are human beings. A cultural revival is one of the ways in which their ethnic history and hence their peoplehood is affirmed. A cultural center, where programs and fellowship are able to cut the umbilical cord with whites, assures them that they are no longer "boys" but "men." I am making the point that Alves needs to take a closer look at the meaning of liberation for blacks over against whites. Once he looks carefully at Harlem and the South Side of Chicago, and examines sources at Howard and Atlanta, he will not so easily equate the causes of the New Left and black militants.

The more constructive contribution of Alves is blunted by the fact that he gets hung up on "technology" at a time when sons and daughters of the greatest military-industrial complex in world history are fed up with its effects upon their lives. They are fleeing the fruits of this system for the simple life of nature. I am also concerned that as a Brazilian he spends so much time dealing with the problems of white middle-class Americans and tells us so little about oppression and dehumanization in Brazil. The book is disappointing in that black scholars know a great deal more about these things than an outsider may ever know. Many blacks have studied under and read behind the same scholars. His real task, as I see it, was to reinterpret the Christian faith in the light of the Brazilian experience. If he had done this well, he would have gone beyond his white teachers and enriched the "theology of oppression." This is the point at which his contribution to black liberation would have been greatest.

In spite of these shortcomings of Alves's book, there are worthy insights that reveal his native sensitivity to oppression. He is writing about a messianic humanism, and not about a humanistic messianism (that is, Marxism). In other words, Alves takes sin, salvation, and divine grace with all seriousness. He does not hope for *our* future, but *God's* future. But insofar as history is related to the status quo, it is not conceived as black history. The black theologian is taking black history seriously because he needs a "cultural home." Alves speaks for a people fleeing colonialism who would like to forget their past and move into a new future. Between Alves and the blacks, there appears to be a "cultural lag." Blacks have sought this future in the white mainstream. What they seek now is still the good life, but on their terms. They must now move back into the past to rediscover their past before moving forward to a future of liberation and reconciliation between equals.

The concept of a messianic humanism is suggestive, nevertheless, of some elements that must be included in a black understanding of hope—present and future. God of the past is in command of the present and the future. No future God, no waiting God, is adequate for our hope. The God of the consummation must be likewise the "God of our weary years" and the "God of our silent tears"—"the one who has brought us this far on the way." We affirm the isness of the wasness of God. We believe that the God who shall be now is, and is a "very present help in trouble."

Alves points to the oppressed as those who understand the language of hope, freedom, and liberation. The oppressed also understand what death is because they experience the death of hopelessness and futurelessness.[2] He asserts that God is found among the powerless, those who suffer. God participates in the weakness and sufferings of the slave. His sufferings are the ground of hope for those who are without hope. There is no glorification of suffering as an end in itself. God suffers with us to set us free.[3] It is helpful to hear Alves stress the point that God is the suffering slave (*doulos*, Phil. 2:7),[4] and that the sufferings of the oppressed are not simply the sufferings of humans but God's suffering as well.[5] But Alves is too futuristic. His teachers have pointed him to the future. Black theologians should be most concerned about their present. Unless something happens in the present, there will be little to hope for in the future—at least in this life.

My purpose for dwelling upon Alves was not to set him up as a straw man, for he is more than that. He is making a signal contribution to contextual theology and ethics. But as far as a doctrine of last things is concerned, he does not help us very much. His mistakes are instructive. He teaches us that we should wean ourselves from our white teachers with haste and reinterpret everything for our own use. On the positive side, he shows us how to work at a theology of oppression even if we disagree on direction and interpretation.

Most recent black scholars have not even concerned themselves with the future. The theme, even of Martin Luther King, Jr., has been "freedom now." Whether this is realistic or not, is not the question. The point of urgency is made. As James Cone states it:

"Freedom Now" has been and still is the echoing slogan of all civil rights groups. The same concept of freedom is presently expressed among Black Power advocates by such phrases as "self-determination" and "self-identity."[6]

Cone expresses real skepticism regarding the future life. He says: "The idea of heaven is irrelevant for Black Theology. The Christian cannot waste time contemplating the next world (if there is a next)."[7]

There is no place, according to Cone, for a reward. Humankind is made free for obedience without "a pat on the back from God."[8] Human beings now know that they are right with God, because God has put them in this state. They are henceforth free to be all for the neighbor. Cone feels that concern for heaven is a denial of freedom. He feels that concern for heaven leads to an undue sense of worth and therefore assures one of favor with God. The free person has no concern for reward in heaven. Through the freedom granted one in Christ, one plunges oneself into the evils of the world. One does not seek salvation, for to seek it is to lose it.[9]

It is interesting that Black Muslims reject belief in eschatology for similar reasons; namely, that the Christian belief in last things is a gambit to keep the black person happy in oppression. But Islam is also an eschatological creed. The denial of the afterlife by the Black Muslims reveals that the movement is more of a Christian heresy reacting to oppression based upon race in this country than it is a sect of classic Islam. It is ironic that James Cone, as Christian theologian, should be in the same camp regarding eschatology.

There is an uncanny inconsistency in Cone between the utter helplessness of a person to do any good thing and the expectation that one be involved in social reconstruction. How is it possible to hold on to human dignity if one is "helpless under God's wrath"?[10] But in speaking of eschatology, Cone does believe God is at work here and now. Cone says:

Black Theology insists that genuine biblical faith relates eschatology to history, that is, to what God has done, is doing, and will do for his people. It is only because of what God has done and is now doing that we can speak meaningfully of the future.[11]

It is my understanding that the only future Cone believes in is our future in this life. Here I must agree with Paul when he says: "If for this life only we have hoped in Christ, we are of all men most to be pitied" (1 Cor. 15:19). An eschatology without a future dimension is only partially complete. It may include the cross, as Cone has done, but it does not include the resurrection.

Black experience is not only "double"—it is "triple." When DuBois speaks of the "doubleness" of black experience, he does not include the destiny of the human spirit or soul. The black person shares humanity with all humans. For example, there are some sufferings of blacks that are shared with all humans because of our psychophysical makeup. There are other sufferings that are reserved for those who are victims of racism in a white society. Finally, there are sufferings that touch the soul and are spiritual in nature.

Psychophysical pain and spiritual suffering belong to all humans as persons simply because "men are not like sheep or goats that nourish a blind life within the brain." It is the victimization of blacks in a white racist society that colors the interpretation of the experience of being human (our dignity) and the hope of the future life (our destiny). To concentrate totally upon our victimization would have to overlook the multidimensional aspects of our experience—especially what we share with all humans. This omission impoverishes both the experience and the communication of our understanding of the unique aspect of our experience to others in relation to whom we are to be liberated and reconciled.

Howard Thurman is a firm believer in a future life. He examines the spirituals and arrives at some important conclusions. For the slave, "death was a fact, inescapable, persistent. . . . It was extremely compelling because of the cheapness with which life was regarded. The slave was a tool, a thing, a utility, a commodity, but he was not a person. He was faced constantly with the imminent threat of death."[12]

Thurman points to the fact that when slaves were killed, their deaths were mere property losses—a matter of bookkeeping. The notion of personality, of human beings as ends, was never considered in the master-slave relationship.[13] Thurman continues:

To live constantly in such a climate makes the struggle for essential human dignity unbearably desperate. The human spirit is stripped to the literal substance of itself. The attitude toward death is profoundly influenced by the experience of life.[14]

Thurman goes on to describe various attitudes concerning death that emerged out of this experience. Sometimes death was considered as a friend. Some things in life are worse than death. This was not a mere counsel of suicide; it was a reflection upon the absence of "an elemental affirmation" of "the dignity of the human spirit" and a "basis for self-respect."[15] Another attitude was "one of resignation mixed with elements of fear and a manifestation of muted dread."[16] Death is also regarded as release—"a complete surcease from anxiety and care." Death is good in itself as "an exulting sigh of sheer release from a very wearying burden." This view does not concern itself with the afterlife.[17]

Thurman turns to life. He made the point that the attitude toward death is based upon the experience of life. Life can be regarded as "an experience of evil, of frustration, of despair."[18] Life is likewise understood by the oppressed black as "a pilgrimage, a sojourn, while the true home of the spirit is beyond the vicissitudes of life with God!"[19] Death, according to Thurman, means complete cessation of events. Life, on the other hand, means movement, process, growth. He finds no meaningful understanding of a before and after in terms of death and life. Thus for him death is something that happens in life. Life that transcends death is "significant because of the advantage that is given to the meaning of life."[20] Thurman sums up his views as follows as he speaks of the blacks who wrote their experiences of suffering in the spirituals:

> To them this quality of life was insistent fact because of that which deep within them, they discovered of God, and his far-flung purposes. God was not through with them. ... To know him was to live a life worthy of the loftiest meaning of life.[21]

Thurman is not a theologian. He is a mystic relying greatly upon philosophy and psychology as means for interpreting religious experience. As a Christian he is greatly inspired by the Jesus of history (the human example of Jesus), by the Spirit (as he empowers the inner life), and by the prophets. His dislike for Paul makes it impossible to deal with the resurrection, which is central to a Christian understanding of the last things. He is inspired by the Quakers (especially Rufus Jones) and blends Hindu mysticism (*advaita*) with the Platonic acknowledgments of the immortality of the soul. He brings East and West together as he deals with the concept of time. "Life," according to Thurman, "becomes illustrative of a theory of time that is latitudinal or flowing" (that is, in the thought of Henri Bergson). He juxtaposes death to life by observing that "death is suggestive of a theory of time that is circular or wheel-like."[22]

Thurman does not present a distinctively "Christian" eschatology, but he does make these important points. First, that the black person's own experience has shaped his or her view of life, death, and the beyond. There is a basis for belief in the future life emerging out of the black person's experience, which is not totally dependent upon the preachment of so-called white Christians. Second, Thurman has made the point that life, death, and the hereafter are interrelated. What one thinks of life relates to what one thinks of death; or the future life beyond death has an impact upon the meaning of life. It follows that even though we are greatly concerned about conditions here and now, we will greatly impoverish our understanding of the Christian faith if we are indifferent to the "not yet" of eschatology.

What those who invest all their hopes in the present life should realize is that the most uncertain thing about life is life itself. Furthermore, a person's life is more than what one eats, where one lives, and where one works. It is perfectly possible to master the how of life and not have a why for living. Blacks who place all their hopes in the present should observe that many whites, who have all the things and success they so greatly desire, are anxious in a pathological sense and their children are on drugs having become dropouts from life itself.

Elsewhere I have made the important point that Jesus was speaking directly to our human condition when he urged us to seek the kingdom of God first (Matt. 6:33). To place material concerns in a position of priority is to "major in minors."[23] In my essay with that title, I discuss four examples of the tendency of Americans (including blacks) to place "accents on accessories" to the neglect of the cultivation of the moral and spiritual dimensions of life. First, we are majoring in quantity and minoring in quality. Second, we are majoring in houses and minoring in homes. Third, we are majoring in knowledge and minoring in wisdom. Fourth, we are majoring in speed and minoring in purpose. When humans preoccupy themselves with the claims of earth to the neglect of the kingdom of God, what we have is "an emptiness, a forlornness, a despair, an aching void."[24]

I believe Augustine was correct: "Thou hast made us for thyself, O God, and our hearts are restless until they find rest in thee." These words of the African bishop, who has influenced all Christian theology, should be taken with all seriousness. Black Theology must say clearly to blacks engaged in a feverish attempt to find fulfillment in "things," that "man does not live by bread alone." It is important that in the Sermon on the Mount, as recorded in Matthew, Jesus prays, "Give us this day our daily bread" (Matt. 6:11) and goes on to raise the question: "Is not life more than food, and the body more than clothing?" (Matt. 6:25). He seems to be saying that life cannot be lived without bread, but life is also more than bread.

Those who see this life as everything do not fully appreciate either human nature or destiny. Human nature as understood through the Christian faith includes the spiritual dimensions of life that cannot be fully understood or fulfilled with reference only to material and temporal existence. We have a higher calling and a higher destiny. We sell black religion short if we believe that the understanding of life and death and the future life was limited to what the slave masters told slaves about the future life. This explains the otherworldly, escapist, or "opiate" understanding of the future life. But it does not do justice to Dr. King's assertion that "if you have something worth living for, you have also something worth dying for." This prophetic or "protest" posture toward death and the future life is equally characteristic of black religion from the beginning.

A Christian does not need to face injustice here and now or death in the context of a skepticism of belief about the future life. It is precisely because the God who offers eternal life is lord of history, and lord over death, that we have a deeper insight into the meaning and the mission of the present life. It is true that white preachers pointed black and oppressed people to heavenly rewards while denying them the expectation of liberation in the here and now. They used this otherworldly version of eschatology to make blacks content with their present lot of bondage and oppression. But this is a distortion of the doctrine of the last things. It is a good reason for a black theologian to do his or her job of reinterpretation in the light of the needs arising out of the black experience, but at the same time seek to be faithful to the biblical revelation. One does not need to "throw the baby out with the bath." This can be said of the entire Christian faith and it is especially true of this important doctrine.

Even if black Christians have not understood the relation between the now and then aspects of eschatology and how they are related, it is the task of the black theologian to enlighten others. I am not surprised that Black Power advocates, uninformed concerning this vital aspect of the Christian faith, who are "cultured despisers" of religion known only to them as an "opiate," denounce the Christian faith as a whole as "whitianity" and the "afterlife" with it. But one speaking as a black theologian (that is, James Cone), as an apologist for the Christian faith in this time of black consciousness and power, has an awesome responsibility to "open up the Scriptures" and interpret "the whole gospel" in reference to the black experience. Insofar as Cone has not connected unrealized and realized eschatology, he has been remiss at this task.

Ethics and eschatology are related in Black Theology. This is the basis of the black hope. This is the bridge between the now and the not yet, the promised and the fulfilled. Reinhold Niebuhr is correct, I believe, in pointing to ethical principles as "possible impossibilities." Our present life is "a political situation" subject to the tension between "reach" and "grasp." Things hoped for and reached after always elude complete fulfillment, but the promises and ideals of the Christian faith inspire us to keep "reaching." Indeed, a Christian dies reaching—"if man's reach does not exceed his grasp, what are the heavens for?" One can be inspired to live and act by what ought to be, but one really lives and acts in the context of what is. This is true even if one gives one's life for what ought to be.

Christian realism can be activistic, political, even revolutionary, in its impact upon personal and social evils. But while being aware of what ought to be, it deals with the possible and moves from one possibility to the next. Absolute demands often die stillborn on the lips of those who make them and are usually ignored by those who have no vested interest in their realization. Empty threats, in the long run, are as bad as false promises— neither lead to fulfillment. I am aware that love is always being crucified in history and thus the need for the pushing and shoving of justice.

Black hope present and future is bound up with an understanding of the kingdom of God as present and future. The kingdom that is "within" is present wherever the will of God is being done. But we are also, as Christians, "heirs of the kingdom which God has promised" (James 2:5). There is a kingdom "not from the world" (John 18:36), which Christians are to inherit (Matt. 25:34). In the time of final reckoning, the now and not yet, the now and then, the present and future, the this-worldly and the other-worldly, ethics and eschatology will be one. In the time of separation of the "sheep" from the "goats," the king will say to the unrepentant and unforgiven: "Depart from me, you cursed, into the eternal fire prepared for the devil and his angels; for I was hungry and you gave me no food, I was thirsty and you gave me no drink" (Matt. 26:41–42).

But to those who are on his right hand, the repentant and forgiven, he will say:

Come, O blessed of my Father, inherit the kingdom prepared for you from the foundation of the world; for I was hungry and you gave me food, I was thirsty and you gave me drink. . . . Then the righteous will answer him, "Lord when did we see thee hungry and feed thee, or thirsty and gave thee drink?" . . . And the King will answer them, "Truly, I say to you, as you did it to one of the least of these my brethren, you did it to me." (Matt. 25:34–40)

We are also aware that before this throne shall be "all the nations"— all humans, black, yellow, white, and red. In the book of Revelation we read: "I looked, and behold, a great multitude . . . from every nation, from all tribes and peoples and tongues, standing before the throne and before the Lamb, clothed in white robes, with palm branches in their hands" (Rev. 7:9).

When, according to this account, the question was asked, Who are these? The answer was: "These are they who have come out of the great tribulation; they have washed their robes and made them white in the blood of the Lamb" (Rev. 7:14).

These further words of assurance are given:

They shall hunger no more, neither thirst any more. . . . For the Lamb in the midst of the throne will be their shepherd, and he will guide them to springs of living water; and God will wipe away every tear from their eyes. (Rev. 7:16–17)

Think of the comfort and assurance these words can bring to the oppressed. They can provide them not merely strength to endure, but courage to oppose every evil. It is to be remembered, however, that the kingdom within and the kingdom of inheritance belong only to those "who have washed their robes and made them white in the blood of the Lamb." Blacks do not possess the kingdom *because* they are black and poor. Whites are not excluded *because* they are white and rich. Only those who know the Christian experience of forgiveness, who have been sanctified (grown in their relation to God in Christ), and who have been led by the Spirit into a life of social concern and action, can be heirs of the kingdom of God. It enriches the Christian life to see the future from a life lived in the power of God's Spirit in the present, and then see the present, from the vantage point of the kingdom that is to come.

Eternal life is a *quality* of life. When compared with the sinful or unrighteous life, it is different in kind as well as in *fullness* or *degree*. Eternal life is the "abundant" life. Heaven, consummation of the Christian experience of forgiveness and sanctification, is not a *space* but a *state*. It has been characteristic for blacks in their songs and sermons to speak of heaven in terms of the best places and things open to the imagination. During slavery, reference was made to the possessions of the master then denied the slave. The Islamic heaven is filled with wine, women, and song. The Native American's heaven is a "happy hunting ground." When persons view the afterlife as "heaven," the imagination stands on tiptoe in order to capture the highest and the best as viewed by believers from their experience. Heaven of experience can be either the continuation of the best or a fulfillment of desires unfulfilled in this life. It is not surprising that longing for "heaven" kept hope alive in "the souls of black folks." Even if this was bad theology, it was good psychology. It was soothing like balm "as it cheered the weary travelers along the heavenly road."

Eternal life is everlasting life. It is an experience, in a conscious sense, "of being with the Lord." It is timelessness. But it is also duration. The experience of eternal life, according to John's Gospel, begins now and continues forever. When one comes to a saving knowledge of God in Christ, the experience of eternal life begins. Death is a "terminal," not the "terminus." It is like opening the door that leads into another room. The Spirit of God is the giver and sustainer of the spiritual life and thus whether we live or die, we live in the Lord. Paul sums it up thus: "For me to live is Christ, and to die is gain" (Phil. 1:21). Paul says he is ready to depart this life and be completed with Christ, but he would like to remain longer in the flesh to labor for his Lord (Phil. 1:22–23).

If heaven is eternal blessedness, hell is eternal separation. If God is the source and sustainer of life, think what it must be like to be estranged from God as boundless love, mercy, and grace. Hell is not a place, but a state of experience. God is the one who "lets be." We owe our lives—physical and spiritual—to God. Hell is other people, only if by our estrangement from God, hell is already present within. When a fallen and perverted human will confronts a holy and just God in defiance, one creates for oneself a "hell." Unfortunately a society of perverted wills may create a "hellish" situation for the oppressed. But the Lord of History who is lovingly just, who is also Judge and the Consummator of all things here and hereafter, does not sleep and has the last word. Black hope is rooted in the faith that the God of the "end time" is also the God of the "present time." God is our present Redeemer as well as our future Judge. This faith has kept hope alive when there was no tangible basis for hope. A people cannot survive without hope. Our faith in God has kept hope alive.

The real basis for hope for all Christians is the resurrection. Paul has given us the classic statement on the central importance of the resurrection to our eternal hope in 1 Corinthians, chapter 15. Without the resurrection, there is no good news to preach and no faith to sustain us. Faith is futile and sins remain unforgiven if there is no resurrection. Without the resurrection, there is no life beyond death. Paul exclaims his faith in the resurrection:

> But in fact the Christ has been raised from the dead, the first fruits of those who have fallen asleep. For as by a man came death, by a man has come also the resurrection of the dead. For as in Adam all die, so also in Christ shall all be made alive. (1 Cor. 15:20–22)

Oscar Cullmann seems to capture the significance of the Christian doctrine of the resurrection when he says:

> In the foreground of the Christian message stand those . . . statements, that Christ is risen, after having conquered powers and authorities, that Christ rules as Lord over all things in heaven and on earth![25]

Thus, Christian hope is based upon the resurrection of the body (somatic-body), not the resurrection of the flesh. The survival and triumph of the holistic self, of the personality, is assured for those who have a saving relationship with Christ, whom God has raised from the dead and has made "both Lord and Christ." This Christocentric view of the resurrection is founded upon the faith of Christians in the crucifixion-resurrection event. It is based upon the faith that the Christian shares the passion, cross, and power of the Lord of Life and Lord over death. Faith in the Christus Victor, "the victorious Christ," is the basis of our hope, as blacks, that both liberation and reconciliation are assured and that meaning and the quest for social justice are proper goals for our lives. "Thanks be to God, who gives us the victory through our Lord Jesus Christ" (1 Cor. 15:57).

8

Bombs and Bullets/Ballots and Bills

Throughout this discussion, I have pointed to ethical concerns from time to time. I have indicated in this manner that theological ethics must be built into a Black Theology. This is true because the Christian faith is moral as well as religious. But it is true, especially for Black Theology, for the reason that moral questions are associated with whether Christianity is suitable for blacks at all. For instance, anti-Christian attitudes or the enchantment with another religion (for example, Islam) are often related to the fact that racism is believed to be an integral part of the Christian faith per se. Exponents of the Christian creed, if they are to overcome this challenge, must "isolate" the Christian faith from racist distortions. The history of the manner in which Christianity has been presented, misused, and applied in the area of race, at home and abroad, is a gigantic hoax. It is "a miracle of grace" that any blacks are still Christians or that they would be convinced of its tenets to such an extent that a few would become scholarly interpreters of its faith and ethics to other blacks, and that many would be proclaimers of the good news of the gospel to the masses of blacks.

While militant blacks, not associated with Christianity, pronounce the death of the black church, the black church itself seems to be gaining ground among the masses. This is especially true if the leader is able to meet spiritual and material needs of the masses at the same time, and show the relationship between the two.

The "death of God" movement passed blacks by. The "church is dead" movement is not true to the black experience either. As a religious people, we need the church. The black church is a "healing" institution for oppressed people, but it is also a "protest" institution. It is the most powerful social and moral institution we have to fight injustice. It is for this reason that I am constantly urging black militants: first, to know the Christian faith and its ethics, and second, if need be, to radicalize the church from the inside rather than to criticize it from the outside. Whatever the black church is not doing may be overcome through vigorous leadership and lay support. The black church has almost unlimited resources for racial uplift and for overcoming the barriers imposed by white racists.

It is important to state presently the goal of black-white relations as I view them against the background of my statement of Black Theology. I do not advocate integration as a goal. Integration is a goal set by whites and is still based upon the superordination-subordination principle of whites over blacks, even blacks with superior education and experience to whites under whom they must live and serve. In any situation where whites write the agenda for integration – whether in government, business, education, industry, even religion – this is what integration means. The slave-master, servant-boss, inferior-superior mentality underlie all integration schemes in which whites write the agenda. This is the reason why I am against integration.

Black and white relations should be interracial. This allows for two-way participation in the interaction between the races. It overcomes the self-hate implicit in the belief that all whites are superior to all blacks just because white is inherently better than black. Positively, it enables blacks to appreciate their own heritage to the extent that they consider it a worthy commodity to be shared with others. In this manner, liberation leads to reconciliation between equals. This position is productive of the psychological and sociological health of blacks. It is needed for a right perspective for better race relations. It is consistent with an understanding of God as lovingly just, the dignity of all persons, the sinfulness of all, and their reconciliation with God and with one another through Jesus Christ.

I am equally opposed to separatism as an end in itself. Separatism is at best only a temporary solution. Just as rugged individualism is giving way to a more socialized economy, and strict nationalism of new nations is melting under the weight of the interdependence of nations in a nuclear age and in the time of world history, even so the days of separatism are numbered in race relations. It is frankly more rhetoric than reality, and it is rather foolish not to be able to see the difference; for we must live or coexist in a multiracial and culturally pluralistic society until and unless we solve the "land" question. It seems that the interracial view offers a more lasting as well as a just solution to the race problem if it can become operative in a massive way. If every merger of black and white institutions can begin with equity as a basis of their union, then we may avoid a lot of undoing and redoing. Henceforth, mergers must be undertaken in such a way as to overcome the powerlessness of blacks. All mergers must be intercultural and based upon equal dignity of all persons involved. A black cultural nationalism can tie into this interracial stance.

In cases where blacks are a tiny minority in a white majority, a fifty-fifty vote is meaningless. Consider the Consultation on Church Union, in which some black Methodists are involved in the proposed Church of Christ Uniting, and these blacks themselves are splintered into four denominations. The other blacks are small caucuses in integrated bodies in which they are swallowed up and in a real sense powerless. This illustrates the need for blacks "to get their thing together" and be in position to bargain for social justice from a position of strength rather than from a position of disunity or weakness. If need be, they should withdraw from the negotiations altogether until such time as they are united. Otherwise, whatever the promises from whites, they will not be able to "bloc vote" with sufficient numbers to make their demands heard.

Furthermore, the destiny of blacks may easily be exploited by whites, who have always used the "divide and rule" principle whenever they wanted to have their own way. If it be said that there is a note of distrust in this judgment, I retort that the record of whites over blacks—even in the church—does not recommend overdue confidence. Therefore, ample safeguards are needed until whites have "lived down" some of their history of the exploitation of blacks.

In all plans, decisions, and execution of programs involving blacks and whites, blacks must operate on the basis of interracial equity. Equity implies the natural and God-given; it is rooted in both nature and grace, and is shared by all persons. Thus, what is equitable cannot be given or taken away by whites. To think and act on this principle is the only means to liberation and the only proper basis for black-white reconciliation.

A black pastor pointed to Amos as a prophet of justice. Amos knew only the wrath of God. The minister wanted to know if the black church should take Amos more seriously. It was his impression that the church is a "do-nothing" institution simply because it is paralyzed by "love." While we are taking Amos with all seriousness, there has to be a place in our understanding of authentic prophecy for Hosea—even for Jesus. There is a moral honestness in Amos that is essential for exposing the seriousness of our inhumanity. Black Theology needs a heavy dose of Amos.

The God of Amos is "an angry God." Amos is a man of the people; he is a "folk" prophet. The masses have been exploited by priests and politicians just as blacks have been. Amos is a prophet of social justice:

> For I know how many are your transgressions,
>   and how great are your sins—
> you who afflict the righteous, who take a bribe,
>   and turn aside the needy in the gate. (Amos 5:12)

Those who exploit the poor and mete out violence to the needy and underprivileged sleep "upon beds of ivory" (Amos 6:4), possess "winter" and "summer" houses (Amos 3:15). They "sell the righteous for silver, and the needy for a pair of shoes" (Amos 2:6). This speaks of punishment, desolation, darkness, and judgment. The God of Amos says:

> I hate, I despise your feasts,
>   and I take no delight in your solemn
>   assemblies. . . .

But let justice roll down like waters,
and righteousness like an ever-flowing stream.
(Amos 5:21, 24)

Recently as I rode with friends through the city of Indianapolis, I noticed a sign over a tractor company: God Bless America. This reminded me of the "God and country" romance going on. The friendship, developing into a national scandal, between Billy Graham and Richard Nixon illustrated this trend. The Honor America Program on July 4, 1970, in which Billy Graham was a chief star, attempted to ignore all the injustices at home and abroad in which this country was so deeply involved. It wanted to sprinkle holy water on "unholy" America. Someone else more honest than all those involved in this unholy alliance of priests and politicians carried a sign on his car: MY COUNTRY, RIGHT or WRONG. This position does at least suggest that America might be wrong, even if there is a general lack of moral perception. The unholy alliance is most deadly because of the power controlled by those involved together with the insensitivity to evil. Like Faustus, they seem to be saying: "Evil, be thou good." At a time when there is too much "piety on the Potomac" of the wrong kind, we need to rediscover the God of Amos — the God of social justice.

But unless we are to fall victim to the Marcionite misunderstanding of God, the God of Amos must also be the God of Hosea. The God of justice is also the God of love and mercy. Hosea is not naive or ignorant of the gravity of the sins of his people: "My people are destroyed for lack of knowledge; because you have rejected knowledge, I reject you" (Hosea 4:6).

And again: "There is no faithfulness or kindness, and no knowledge of God in the land" (Hosea 4:1). God is a gracious God to Hosea. Where there is repentance, there is forgiveness:

Come, let us return to the Lord;
for he has torn, that he may heal us;
he has stricken, and he will bind us up. (Hosea 6:1)

There is no lack of judgment in the prophecy of Hosea. He condemns internal sins (the sins among his people) as well as external sins (sins of another people). But he continually reminds Israel that God is the God of the exodus. A cardinal attribute of the God of Hosea is *hesed*, "steadfast love":

I will destroy you, O Israel;
who can help you? . . .
The iniquity of Ephraim is bound up,
his sin is kept in store. (Hosea 13:9, 12)

In words that anticipate the Christus Victor gospel of the resurrection of 1 Corinthians, chapter 15, Hosea exclaims:

> Shall I ransom them from the power of Sheol?
>   Shall I redeem them from Death?
> O Death, where are your plagues?
>   O Sheol, where is your destruction? . . .
> I will heal their faithfulness;
>   I will love them freely,
>   For my anger has turned from them.
>   (Hosea 13:14, 14:4)

Though God is merciful, God is likewise just:

> The ways of the Lord are right,
>   and the upright walk in them,
>   but transgressors stumble in them. (Hosea 14:9)

One observes in Martin Luther King, Jr., this blend of justice and love. Amos and Jesus are prophetic models for King. A worthy understanding of the Christian God and God's moral requirements must include justice and mercy, judgment and forgiveness. Jonah knew only of the wrath of God and was surprised that God saved repentant Nineveh (Jonah 4:1–3). Micah, on the other hand, understood that God is lovingly just. Therefore, according to Micah, God requires us "to do justice, and to love kindness, and to walk humbly with God" (Micah 6:8).

Dr. King, I believe, had a sound grasp of biblical ethics—one that will win in the long run. It is my understanding that he leaned too far, at first, toward love as an ethical norm. He accepted Aulen's interpretation of *agape* uncritically. Therefore, his understanding of love was not always as robust as it might have been. But because the shadow of Amos, the prophet of social justice, forever haunted him, King never allowed love to become sentimentality. The later King, when confronted with Black Power, became more and more like Amos. He became more militant and thus even love became a means to racial injustice. He was pushed by the logic of events to the very edge of violence. His brinkmanship was so pronounced that even though he did not advocate violence, he created a climate in which violence sprang to the surface. He insistently made the point that his program was the only alternative to violence, thus perhaps unwittingly contributing to the racial fears that breed violence.

King's dream was for a promised land of integration—one in which blacks would be admitted to white society with everything to receive, with little if anything to give. King's utopia has been shattered by the realism of subsequent events. Whites must understand that this is due as much, if not more, to the white backlash as it is to the emergence of Black Power. The state of accommodation to the superordination-subordination model of race relations moved into a phase of conflict and confrontation because blacks were no longer willing to buy a system that victimized them with indignity and inferiority. The calm was broken because there was no real indication that whites intended a radical break with the status quo. Thus when the "magnolia myth" of the contented black was broken by angry mobs of blacks during the "long hot summers," whites longed for the good old days and wondered what had happened to all the "good niggers"—those who had for so long accommodated themselves to inhuman treatment.

One of the most serious dilemmas facing black Christians in their period of black-white confrontation is the question of means. While certain revolutionary theologians advocate violence or counterviolence in Latin America and South Africa, the "by whatever means necessary" ethic needs careful examination by black theologians and ethicists. It may be loudly applauded by black militants who have an ear for inflammatory rhetoric, but it will hardly do for a sound Christian basis for ethics in the area of race. The proper approach is to describe and seek a deeper understanding of ethical directives rather than merely to use the Bible to sanction what Black Power advocates have arrived at by instinct alone. Given the history of violence in this society and the inhuman treatment to which blacks have been subject, hate and violence are indeed the most natural response. Fortunately, we must press on to seek the proper Christian response if we have anything worth saying at all.

At a memorial service for the students killed at Jackson State, one black minister advocated radical economic, social, and political measures to right the wrongs in the area of race. He admonished students to use their time, energy, and talents to work for the cause for which those students died. Another black minister denounced all forms of nonviolence as a means to radical change in the area of race. He despaired of any effectiveness stemming from the most radical forms of militant nonviolence. His proposed solution was "bullets" alone. In his view, all blacks must now be willing to die for the cause. He denounced the church and made it known that his ministry was meaningless to him, that if he were not a pastor, he would not attend church. The church, for his part, was only a power base for action— a means to an end. This contrast of ethical ideology and program is representative of the confusion facing the black religious leadership both lay and clerical. The fact is that blacks have tried all types of ideologies and programs of action against racial injustice, and the result has been a mere dent in the wall of discrimination. It is not difficult to understand why so many have given up on whites and why there is such moral confusion on such questions as violence or nonviolence in black-white confrontation.

When I mentioned nonviolence as the only moral, pragmatic, and Christian means to racial betterment in Chicago during the summer of 1966, I was stunned by the bitter response of some of my best ministerial friends. They reminded me that what I had just said was quite dangerous and that it was good that I had first mentioned this among friends. They went on to relate how they had participated in nonviolent work, but they now were aware that nonviolence was finished, simply because it did not move the wills of whites to liberate blacks. On the deepest level they felt that nonviolence was somehow more Christian than violence, even though some were then becoming suspicious of the white ethicists who had taught them. But even if they were personally convinced that "love is the more excellent way," they wondered why blacks, as Christians, are expected to be so moral, while whites are so immoral. Since nonviolence had failed, they had begun to put their trust in violence. Some agreed that nonviolence was Christian, but they had noted already that whites were now willing to do something, whereas in the past they had ignored their peaceful protests. Now that angry black militants bent on violence were taking over the leadership, whites were seeking out ministers with the hope that they could still calm the masses. They hoped that White Power would be used in a wholesale manner to right the wrongs among blacks, to keep these violent leaders from taking things completely out of their hands.

These ministers still believed in reconciliation, but they knew that liberation of the blacks must now come first. After a few years, many of these religious leaders have second thoughts. Instead of massive programs to correct the injustices among blacks, they have witnessed too often bloody repression by the white power structure. Bombs and bullets have thus far been rather a demonstration of the powerlessness of blacks than a demonstration of power. If some black scholars believe violence to be *theologically* sound, events have proven violence to be *pragmatically* and *psychologically* bad for blacks. To see people who participated in riots and looting in a "soup line" and as objects of "white charity" is an empty victory for advocates of violence as the only viable means to racial betterment.

Violence takes more than one form. There is covert violence as well as overt violence. Blacks suffer from both forms of violence. Covert violence is subtle and insidious. Whites often participate in this form of violence without knowing it. If they do not participate in it to a great extent, they permit it to happen without using their influence to end it. The treatment of persons as things is a form of violence. The economic and political exploitation of blacks is a form of violence. Often the best way for whites to help blacks is not to join Black Power, but to curb and redirect White Power. Not to do anything is not merely an indication of insensitivity or indifference; whites who do nothing to curb covert violence are guilty of the sin of omission. So many so-called white Christians are quick to condemn the rioting and looting of blacks, who out of sheer frustration born of despair become destructive in an open manner, without seeking to remove the root causes of the despair, deep frustrations, and dashed hopes of the blacks.

Overt violence is and has been the experience of blacks. Self-hatred, which is sustained by lack of appreciation for themselves, causes them to inflict pain upon one another. Exploitation is internal as well as external to the black community. While a great deal of this may be explained by the fallenness of humanity, the problem is aggravated by the effect of racism upon blacks. Blacks, because of racism, have learned to hate themselves and hate others in black skin. The desire of selfish gain is heightened by the fact that so little is available to blacks, in money or opportunity. The whites, who control everything worth mentioning — except the black church, black fraternal organizations, and black press — allow only one black person at a time to squeeze beneath the chicken wire. Thus, the black person bent on success becomes an opportunist who is skilled in using blacks and whites alike for his or her own advancement.

Black church persons and black scholars are no exception. As soon as blacks are relieved of the stranglehold of the white establishment, the black establishment attempts to take over. A few blacks, who are either operating from within white institutions or who are funded by whites, set themselves up as kingmakers. They seek out their friends, those who think as they think, or those subject to their control, rather than the most talented and most prepared people among blacks, for the plums they now control. The masses of blacks receive little benefit from these blacks concerned only with feathering their own nests and exalting their friends. Whites who really desire to improve race relations will do well to be on the lookout for the new "establishment" blacks. They should conduct their own talent hunt among blacks, judging each candidate on his or her own merit. This form of internal violence can do little harm to those blacks who are mature, but it can obviously create despair among the young. If Black Power is to be constructive among blacks, it must be used to put an end to the type of internal violence just described.

While the black person, as a Christian, must be self-critical (this includes oneself as well as other blacks), one must never lose sight of the real opponent, the white racist. It is the overt violence of whites that has crippled blacks emotionally as well as physically. The pain inflicted upon blacks both on slave ships and in the dark ghettos makes one of the darkest chapters in the history of the human race. The lynching, beating, and maiming of blacks have been "a popular sport" of respectable "God-fearing" white citizens of America, North and South, throughout the history of this republic. The killing of blacks by blacks and the killing by whites has been little noticed in law or custom.

The myth of the purity of the white race has been channeled through the myth of the purity of the white woman. The accusation of assault, rape, sometimes even a look of desire of a black man directed at a white woman, could be the basis for justifiable homicide by any white man. The character of the woman did not figure into the decision at all. Blacks had no legal or police protection. In the meantime, white men took black women as mistresses at will, and even separated husbands and wives in order to satisfy their animal appetite. Many who are deeply involved in open violence against blacks, even good family men, churchmen and respected citizens in the white community now proclaim themselves as good law-and-order people, as God and country advocates and a part of the silent majority that have been overlooked in the stride toward racial justice. They consider anything done to improve the black person's plight as a barrier to their own freedom. They do not understand why blacks are angry, even violently angry.

Now every black person who remembers his or her past and knows the present understands the anger, frustration, even the violence of blacks in the protest against injustice. All who understand do not advocate violent protest. I happen to believe that violence is pragmatically wrong-headed. Violence usually begets violence, and our foe is infinitely more capable of inflicting pain and destruction than we are. Even gains based on fear of violence are spotty, temporary, and superficial. Whites who respond to violence do so negatively rather than constructively. If they operate by the crisis-response motive, they do just enough to stop the violence and await the next wave of violence.

What we need is a constructive, deeply motivated, long-range, massive reorientation in black-white relations. Only "crusaders without violence" can heal as well as disrupt and destroy. Even blacks themselves are not safe in the hands of those who hate sufficiently to destroy whites. Hate is blind whether it comes from blacks or whites. Violence does not meet even the pragmatic test. Pragmatism holds that "truth is workability." The workability of violence as a means to a better position for blacks is in question. As one who has seen the stark face of racial violence in several major cities and observed close up the tragic aftermath for blacks (even at the hands of their own soul brothers and sisters), I have yet to be convinced of the pragmatic test of violence.

Violence, I believe, is inconsistent with the Christian ethic. Here I condemn violence that is covert or overt, violence of blacks against blacks, and violence of whites against blacks. For this reason, I do not believe that it is all right for blacks to be violent to whites *because* whites have been violent to blacks. Here, as in all instances, "two wrongs will not make a right"; for between right and wrong there is a difference of kind, and not merely of degree. Those who argue for counterviolence, even self-defense, encourage the hatemongers, black and white. Blacks who speak of counterviolence do not distinguish between covert and overt violence. They, therefore, would justify the most rampant form of overt violence as repayment for the violence of whites against blacks, whether overt or covert. There have been and are situations in our world in which violent revolution may be the lesser of two evils and the only path to liberation for millions of humans. The history of such violent upheavals indicates that the masses seldom profit from the wholesale slaughter, and injustice merely changes hands. The nonviolent revolution led by Gandhi in India and the several bloodless coups in Pakistan are far more productive. I understand Nat Turner's insurrection and Bonhoeffer's plot to assassinate Hitler as springing from righteous indignation—as the only obvious path open to freedom and justice for millions. The cases of South Africa and some Latin American countries have given rise to "theologies of revolution" in which naked violence is proposed as being divinely ordered.

If violence of this type is ever consistent with Christian ethics, it will need to be programed and measured. It should be a means rather than an end. It should be used only after all better alternatives have been duly tried and it should be used only because it is the lesser of two evils. As dark as the racial conflict is in this country, I do not believe that we face a situation as bleak as slavery, death camps, or even South Africa. There is still enough goodwill among blacks and whites to seek out more constructive progress in racial understanding and the removal of injustices against blacks. Our understanding of God, humanity, and the moral life requires us to seek out the very best means to overcome racial strife. The matter is urgent and it is serious.

The only thing necessary for evil to take over is for good people (black and white) to do nothing. A great deal depends upon what whites will do as well as what blacks will not do. Blacks can no longer tolerate conditions as they are, having affirmed their dignity. It is not the wise thing for whites to counsel blacks to be patient, but to move White Power to correct the hurt and the wrongs visited too long upon blacks. Blacks must be liberated. There is no shortcut to reconciliation that does not pass through liberation. There can be no reconciliation that does not include equity.

If reconciliation is a proper Christian goal, and I am convinced it is, then violence that destroys the one who is a party to the reconciliation is not a good means. There can be no reconciliation between the dead—at least, not in this life. Violence begets violence rather than goodwill. The result of violence can only be a bloodbath that will be self-defeating as well as self-destructive for blacks. And even though such "black rage" could seriously disrupt the entire nation, it would not be productive of the ends that are being sought in the struggle.

Some have pointed to Jesus' driving the moneychangers out of the temple as an illustration establishing the fact that our Lord did not reject violence as means, given adequate provocation. This righteous anger expressed by Jesus did not include taking the life of the moneychangers. Indeed, Jesus showed us how to hate sin and love the sinner. He told us about love of enemies and limitless forgiveness of the penitent. Paul told us to overcome evil with good and assured us that love is the more excellent way. I submit that we would need to use the Bible rather than interpret it as followers of Christ, to find any real sanction for the kind of violence advocated by some black militants, even ministers and theologians. Violence may offer some promise as means for those who seek only liberation for blacks. Even here I believe their victory would be empty and short-lived. But the "whole gospel" in race relations must never rest with separation as an end in itself. The black person is not to be liberated and separated, but liberated and reconciled. The same applies to whites. The liberating gospel is also a reconciling gospel. It brings us together. In Christ there is no black or white — all are one in him.

When the Jackson State killings aroused the Howard University students, a mature student, who was violently militant two years earlier, advised the students to use political action rather than violence to honor the dead brothers. He reasoned that whites would expect and welcome violence on the Howard campus in order to carry out a massive program of brutal repression. It is encouraging to see young blacks begin to think through and plan for the most effective and moral means to liberation. Within days a city election took place in Alexandria, Virginia. The black candidate for the city council was the first since Reconstruction and the best qualified on the ballot. The killing of a black teenager by a white policeman had caused a mini-riot lasting several nights. The minister who delivered the eulogy for the black boy drank deep from the Christian faith and ethics. In seeking to comfort a sorrowing black community, he was given words of wisdom for those troubled times. A black minister and a white minister had walked through the streets seeking to "cool" the situation. Another minister, a violent militant, had asked "everyone who can stand up under a gun to go and get one." But the black minister who spoke at the funeral urged the people not to use bullets, but ballots. He reminded them that voting, bloc voting, was far more important for their cause than any senseless killings of blacks and whites. This man of God became an agent of reconciliation. While holding up the need for liberation, he dared to preach a gospel of reconciliation. His faith was justified.

The black candidate was elected with many white votes, together with the votes of masses of blacks who voted for the first time. One of the first victories of the black councilman was that he was able to "open up" the council meeting to the public. It will be difficult for white racists to "do their thing" behind closed doors now. The entire population will now know what is being discussed and the decisions controlling their destiny. This is the kind of Black Power that I believe can be fully supported by Christian ethics. It liberates the black person while it leaves the way open for reconciliation between persons of goodwill, whether black or white.

I understand Christian social ethics to include social relations as well as theological ethics. It is important for one seeking a theological ethic to match the black experience to be guided by many disciplines. Biblical ethics, church history, moral philosophy, as well as the history and interpretation of doctrine, will serve as background and provide principles to be applied. The context of decision is black-white confrontation. The legacy of suffering and exploitation endured by blacks and the Africanisms that have shaped their outlook as they have survived and found meaning under these adverse conditions must figure largely in the quest for a theological ethic for black Christians.

Our problem is serious; our ethics must be carefully pondered. The Christian faith has never, under any circumstances, sanctioned "any means" as an ethical program. Blacks will do themselves a disservice if they embrace such relativism, whether they be Christian or not. We need to know how to decide and what to decide for. We need to know what is a proper goal and how best to obtain it. We need to know what is best in the short run and what is best in the long run. We need to know the greatest good for the greatest number of blacks. As moralists we need to consider the relationship between motives, means, and ends. As Christians we need to know how best to recover our dignity and freedom as citizens and children of God, and we need to discover the way not only to coexistence with whites, but of reconciliation as well.

Even though Jesus and Paul do not provide a *prescription* for black-white relations, they do point out *principles* that we may apply. We need the "hindsight" of the prophets, Jesus, Paul, the church through the ages, black history, black culture, and the moral insights of the ages to inform us concerning what we as members of the church and followers of the Christ ought to do as blacks at this time and place.

The task of the black theologian is to present and interpret the Christian ideology for moving Christians to act responsibly to right the wrongs and to heal the hurts in black-white relations. When Kenneth Clark gave a lecture at Swarthmore College, he spoke of humanizing education. He said many things I would have said as a theologian. When we talked later about religion, he said "religion" is what he was talking about. I did not counter this, for there was not time for a discussion. If he meant religion by what he said, it was "the religion of humanity." Humanism is not necessarily Christian humanism, just as moral philosophy is not identical with Christian ethics. When Jesus asked his hearers, What do you do more than others?, he was making this important point. Knowledge of moral philosophy and social relations is important for Christian ethics. The knowledge of God, humanity, sin, forgiveness, and reconciliation are more important, for without reconciliation there is no Christian or theological ethics. Not merely self-realization on a do-it-yourself basis, but God-realization (including reconciliation with the self and the other) through cooperation between human agency and divine grace are important.

Black Power informed by Christian ethics must now move against institutional racism as well as individual racists. The awareness of this need has led many pastors not only into social welfare but into banking and politics. Recently I spoke to a former student of mine who combines his role as pastor with a seat on a city council. I became aware of how much his exposure to theological ethics meant as he voted for or against bills regulating the lives of all citizens in his city. He was more sensitive to the impact of decisions upon human life than others who were controlled by economic and purely pragmatic considerations. Furthermore, his influence and his clarification of the moral questions and humane considerations often led other councilors to humanize their decisions. This led me to suggest that black seminarians need to learn political science, economics, and law, as well as human relations and theology. This new emphasis would not be designed to tone down theological ethics but to enable future black pastors to put these imperatives of the gospel within the context of decision. As leaders of the black church, they would then be able to bring massive pressure to bear upon racist institutions, thus removing the barriers to the good life for teeming multitudes of blacks.

Compassion to our Lord meant healing the sick, exorcising demons, curing the lame, the halt, and the blind. The Christian ethical meaning of compassion is "love in action." Political economy, the use of ballots and of bills (both money and legislation), are suitable means of action for individual Christians and the black church to humanize life for long-suffering black people. While the Black Manifesto moves the religious institutions to fund empowerment programs for blacks as "reparations" for the ills of racism, other institutions with even greater political and economic power must be summoned into what Whitney Young calls a domestic Marshall Plan to put an end to racial injustice in this country. It is my understanding that Black Theology, as it expresses itself through ethical thought and action, supports a program of liberation of blacks, which uses ballots and bills rather than bombs and bullets. Theological ethics would have as its goal black liberation and black-white reconciliation with equity as the bond of the new relationship.

For blacks the social gospel of the "contemporaneous Christ" based upon the "humanity of God" as manifest through the symbol of the black Messiah is more important than any restatement of Gandhian thought. All that we need for a theological ethic is inherent in the message and mission of Jesus as the Christ. Martin Luther King, Jr., was correct in observing that Jesus gave him the message and Gandhi gave him the method. King, nevertheless, went outside the culture of blacks in dwelling upon Gandhi. Few blacks feel any kinship or possess any real knowledge of Indian religion and ethics. Most blacks have not heard of the Gita; they have been nourished on the Bible. Furthermore, Indian religious nationalism is so different from black religious nationalism that any real parallel would be difficult to establish. Black Theology will be wise to forge its ethics from the Bible with the Afro-American experience as the context for thought and action. As one who has spent several years studying and teaching Hinduism, I have a deep appreciation for the Indian religious heritage. What I am raising here is the question of relevance.

Africa rather than India is the black person's cultural home. Christianity rather than Hinduism is the religion with which masses of blacks are most knowledgeable. While King, by thought, example, and life, left a great ethical legacy, it is important that the black theologian work out a theological ethic informed by biblical ethics and the black heritage using language and ideas familiar to the black masses. While this approach will aid external communication, it will likewise further external communication with whites who share the Euro-American and Christian aspects of our heterodox culture. Who among mortals can criticize what a Gandhi or a King did or did not do or understand? It is a miracle of human history that two moral giants of such stature, of two of the great world faiths, appeared during the same century in East and West, and shared so much in thought, life, and action. Nevertheless, it is for black theologians to address the present situation out of their best understanding of the ethical imperatives of the Christian faith.

Finally, we must mention the ethical possibilities of black ecumenism. Here I do not have in mind the Consultation on Church Union. There is real potential in the witness of the National Committee of Black Christians. Black consciousness and the moral use of Black Power for the humanization of blacks have united black churches and Christians who have never worshiped or worked together before. In this unity there is strength for the good of black people. We must not discount the witness of those in black caucuses—militant blacks in white churches. Blacks must not allow whites to salve their consciences through reparations. Too many whites are pleased to be rid of the black presence by funding some empowering project in the black community. These are Christian colonizers who will use separatism to strengthen their racist program. Blacks in white churches must be "plagues on the houses" of white racists who desire to be at ease in Zion while racial injustices continue. Our quest for a theological ethic must provide the ethical imperatives that will lead the church, black and white, to be the church—a liberating and reconciling church.

Notes

1. Theological Discourse in Black

1. James M. Robinson and John B. Cobb, Jr. (eds.), *New Frontiers in Theology: The New Hermeneutic* (Harper & Row, 1964), pp. 6-7.
2. Charles Long, "The Black Reality: Toward a Theology of Freedom," *Criterion* (Spring-Summer 1964), p. 4.
3. Richard N. Soulen, "Black Worship and Hermeneutic," *Christian Century* (Feb. 11, 1970), p. 171.
4. James H. Cone, *Black Theology and Black Power* (Seabury Press, 1969), pp. 1–4.

2. Liberation and Reconciliation

1. Einar Billing, quoted by Richard Shaull, "Liberal and Radical in an Age of Discontinuity," *Christianity and Crisis*, vol. 29, no. 23 (Jan. 5, 1970), p. 343.
2. Gerhard von Rad, *Old Testament Theology*, vol. 2 (Harper & Row, 1966), p. 58.
3. Shaull, "Liberal and Radical," p. 344.
4. Bruce O. Boston, "How Are Revelation and Revolution Related?" *Theology Today*, vol. 26, no. 2 (July 1, 1969), 142.
5. Ibid., p. 147.
6. Kenneth Clark, in the *New York Times*, April 21, 1970, 31.
7. Ibid.
8. Ibid.
9. Ibid.
10. Whitney Young, "Working Together for Our Common Humanity," *Religious Education* (March-April 1970), 142.
11. Waldo Beach, "A Theological Analysis of Race Relations," in Paul Ramsey (ed.), *Faith and Ethics* (Harper & Brothers, 1957), p. 209.
12. Alvin Pitcher, "White Racism and Black Development," *Religious Education* (March-April 1970), 84.
13. Ibid., 85.
14. Ibid., 87.
15. Ibid.
16. Ibid., 88.
17. Ibid.
18. Ibid., 87.
19. From Joseph R. Washington, Jr.'s, unpublished paper "How Black Is Black Religion?" 24, read at the Georgetown University conference on black church/black theology, May 3, 1969.

20. Ibid., 24 f.

21. Ibid., 25.

22. Ibid.

23. Joseph R. Washington, Jr., *Black and White Power Subreption* (Beacon Press, 1969), 116–68.

24. Ibid., 120.

25. See Charles Long, "The Black Reality: Toward a Theology of Freedom," *Criterion* (Spring-Summer 1969), 2.

26. Ibid., 4.

27. Ibid., 5.

28. Ibid., 2.

29. Ibid., 5.

30. Ibid., 6.

31. Addison Gayle (ed.), *Black Expression* (Weybright & Talley), pp. 296–311.

32. Nathan Scott, "Response to Charles Long's Paper," *Criterion* (Spring-Summer 1969), 10.

33. Ibid., 10–11.

34. Ibid., 11.

35. Ibid.

3. Search for Black Peoplehood

1. Richard L. Rubenstein, *After Auschwitz: Radical Theology and Contemporary Judaism* (Bobbs-Merrill, 1966).

2. Joseph R. Washington, Jr., *The Politics of God* (Beacon Press, 1969), p. 155.

3. Albert Cleage, *The Black Messiah* (Sheed & Ward, 1969), p. 274.

4. Ibid., p. 66.

5. Ibid., p. 24.

6. Ibid., pp. 39–47, passim.

7 Ibid., p. 72; cf. 253, 276, 277.

8. Based upon a conversation with a very reliable black student at Swarthmore College during my visiting professorship, 1969–1970.

9. See E. Franklin Frazier, *The Negro Family in the United States* (University of Chicago Press, 1969). Cf. Andrew Billingsley, *Black Families in White America* (Prentice-Hall, 1968). Frazier's study was first published in 1939. The Billingsley study is more contemporary. It has the further advantage of speaking directly to the issues raised in the controversial Moynihan Report of 1965.

10. See Paul Bohannan, *Africa and Africans* (Natural History Press, 1964), pp. 158–73.

11. Billingsley, *op. cit.*, pp. 39–40.

12. Richard Clagett, "Public Sale of Slaves," document dated Tuesday, March 5, 1833, at 1:00 P.M., concerning sale at Potters Mart, Charleston, South Carolina.

13. Bohannan, *Africa*, 159.

14. W.E.B. DuBois, *The Souls of Black Folk* (Fawcett Publications, 1968), p. 142.

15. Ibid., p. 143.

16. Albert Knudson, *Principles of Christian Ethics* (Abingdon-Cokesbury Press, 1943), p. 195.

17. Ibid.

18. Ibid.

19. Ibid.

20. Kenneth Grayston, "Family," in Alan Richardson (ed.), *A Theological Word Book of the Bible* (Macmillan, 1953), pp. 76–79.

4. The God of Black People

1. Herbert H. Farmer, *God and Men* (Abingdon-Cokesbury Press, 1947), and *The World of God* (London: James Nibet, 1955).

2. Benjamin E. Mays, *The Negro's God* (August Meier, general editor, Studies in American Negro Life) (Atheneum, 1968), and *Disturbed About Man* (John Knox Press, 1969). Cf. Martin Luther King, Jr., *The Measure of a Man* (United Church Press, 1968), and George D. Kelsey, *Racism and the Christian Understanding of Man* (Charles Scribner's Sons, 1965).

3. See R.E. Gordon, K.K. Gordon, and Max Gunther, *The Split-Level Trap* (Dell, 1962).

4. During the academic year 1969–1970, I was Visiting Professor of Religion at Swarthmore College. This gave me the opportunity to observe a large sample of students of this type.

5. Vincent Harding, in Mays, *The Negro's God*, from the Preface to the Atheneum edition.

6. Mays, *The Negro's God*.

5. Humanity, Sin, and Forgiveness

1. John Hope Franklin, *From Slavery to Freedom* (Vintage Books, 1969), pp. 265–70.

2. Mays, *Disturbed About Man*, p. 139.

3. Ibid.

4. Kelsey, *Racism and the Christian Understanding of Man*, p. 177.

5. Ibid.

6. Washington, *The Politics of God*, pp. 31–46.

7. King, *The Measure of a Man*, pp. 21–22.

8. Ibid., pp. 28–29.

9. DuBois, *The Souls of Black Folk*, p. xiv.

10. Cone, *Black Theology and Black Power*, pp. 11–12.

11. Paul Tillich, *The Courage to Be* (Yale University Press, 1962), pp. 40–41, 155–56.

12. The following account of "forgiveness" is greatly dependent upon N.H. Snaith, "Forgiveness," in Richardson (ed.), *A Theological Word Book of the Bible*, pp. 85–86. The excellent treatment of H.R. Mackintosh has been extremely helpful. See his *The Christian Experience of Forgiveness* (London: James Nisbet, 1947).

6. The Black Messiah

1. "Symbol," *Webster's Seventh New Collegiate Dictionary* (G. & C. Merriam Company, 1967).

2. Ibid.

3. Garth Gillian, "Language, Meaning, and Symbolic Presence," *International Philosophical Quarterly*, vol. 9, no. 3 (Sept. 1969), 444.

4. Edwyn Bevan, *Symbolism and Belief* (Beacon Press, 1938), p. 11.

5. "Myth," *Webster's Seventh New Collegiate Dictionary.*

6. Charles H. Long (ed.), *Alpha: Myths of Creation* (George Braziller, 1963), pp. 11–12.

7. Ibid., p. 12.

8. Ibid., pp. 13f.

9. Ibid., p. 13.

10. Ibid.

11. Ibid., p. 15.

12. Susanne K. Langer, *Philosophy in a New Key* (New American Library, 1949), p. 143.

13. Vincent Harding, "Black Power and the American Christ," *Christian Century* (Jan. 4, 1967), pp. 13–14.

14. Dr. Kurt F. Leidecker, "The Buddha Image," *Bulletin of the Washington Friends of Buddhism*, vol. 13, no. 5 (Feb. 1970).

15. James Cone has treated this matter in his *Black Theology and Black Power*, pp. 34–43. The best treatment of "Jesus as Liberator" known to me is an unpublished paper by Dr. Joseph A. Johnson, Jr., bishop of the Christian Methodist Episcopal Church. The paper is based upon an address given at the Autumn 1969 Convocation of Andover Newton Theological School.

16. Cone, *Black Theology*, p. 35.

17. Johnson, *loc. cit.*, p. 86.

18. Ibid.

19. Ibid., p. 90.

20. Ibid., p. 91.

21. Ibid.

22. Ibid.

23. Ibid.

24. E. D. Burton, quoted by Edwin McNeil Poteat, *The Scandal of the Cross* (Harper & Brothers, 1928), p. 79.

25. Albert Schweitzer, *The Quest of the Historical Jesus*, tr. by W. Montgomery (London: Adam & Charles Black, 1911), p. 401.

26. Johnson, *loc. cit.*, p. 94.

7. Hope—Now and Then

1. Rubem A. Alves, *A Theology of Human Hope* (Corpus Books, 1969), pp. 128–30.

2. Ibid., p. 114.

3. Ibid., p. 117.

4. Ibid.

5. Ibid., p. 118.

6. Cone, *Black Theology*, p. 39.

7. Ibid., p. 125.

8. Ibid.

9. Ibid.

10. Ibid.

11. Ibid., p. 126.

12. Howard Thurman, *The Negro Spiritual Speaks of Life and Death* (Harper & Brothers, 1947), p. 13.

13. Ibid., p. 14.

14. Ibid., p. 15.

15. Ibid., pp. 15–16.

16. Ibid., p. 17.

17. Ibid., pp. 22–23.

18. Ibid.

19. Ibid., p. 32.

20. Ibid., pp. 32–33, 17.

21. Ibid., p. 56.

22. Ibid., pp. 33. For further discussion on Thurman, see my essay "The American Negro's Contribution to Religious Thought," in Joseph S. Roucek and Thomas Kiernan (eds.), *The Negro Impact on Western Civilization* (Philosophical Library, 1970), pp. 86–89.

23. J. Deotis Roberts, "Majoring in Minors," *The Link* (Sept. 1962), 5–8.

24. Ibid., 8.

25. Oscar Cullmann, *Christ and Time*, tr. by Floyd V. Filson (London: SCM Press, 1952), p. 211.

Select Bibliography

Billingsley, Andrew. *Climbing Jacob's Ladder*. New York: Simon and Schuster, 1992.

Boesak, Allan A. *Black and Reformed*. Edited by Leonard Sweetman. Maryknoll, N.Y.: Orbis, 1984.

Cannon, Katie G. *Black Womanist Ethics*. Atlanta: Scholars Press, 1988.

Collins, Patricia. *Black Feminist Thought*. New York: Routledge, 1991.

Cone, James H. *For My People*. Orbis, 1984.

Evans, James H., Jr. *We Have Been Believers*. Minneapolis: Fortress, 1991.

Felder, Cain H. *Troubling Biblical Waters*. Orbis, 1989.

———, ed. *Stoney the Road We Trod*. Fortress, 1991.

Grant, Jacquelyn. *White Women's Christ and Black Women's Jesus*. Scholars Press, 1989.

Harris, James H. *Pastoral Theology: A Black Church Perspective*. Fortress, 1991.

Hopkins, Dwight N. and George Cummings, eds. *Cut Loose Your Stammering Tongue*. Orbis, 1991.

Hopkins, D.N. *Black Theology U.S.A. and South Africa*. Orbis, 1989.

Jones, Major J. *The Color of God*. Macon, Ga.: Mercer University Press, 1987.

Mosala, Itumeleng J. *Biblical Hermeneutics and Black Theology in South Africa*. Grand Rapids, Mich.: W.B. Eerdmans, 1989.

Roberts, J. Deotis. *Black Theology in Dialogue*. Philadelphia: Westminster Press, 1987.

Walker, Theodore, Jr. *Empower the People*. Orbis, 1991.

West, Cornel. *Race Matters*. Boston: Beacon Press, 1993.

Witvliet, Theo. *The Way of the Black Messiah*. Oak Park, Ill.: Meyer-Stone Books, 1987.

Young, Harry J. *Hope in Process*. Fortress, 1990.

Young, Josiah U., III. *Black and African Theologies*. Orbis, 1986.

Index